Volleyball Training

Volleyball Training

Stuart Biddle
Anne de Looy
Peter Thomas
Rob Youngs

The Crowood Press

First published in 1989 by
The Crowood Press Ltd
Ramsbury, Marlborough
Wiltshire SN8 2HR

New edition 1995

British Library Cataloguing in Publication Data

A catalogue record for this book is available from the British Library.

ISBN 1-85223-880-1

Acknowledgements
Line Illustrations for Chapter 1 by Vanetta Joffe

Typeset by Qualitext Typesetting, Abingdon, Oxon.
Printed in Great Britain by The Bath Press

Contents

THE AUTHORS

Dr STUART BIDDLE: Stuart is a senior lecturer in the School of Education, University of Exeter, where he is the course director of the MSc degree in Exercise and Sport Psychology and president of the European Federation of Sport Psychology. He is an active consultant in sport and exercise and was formerly an international weightlifting competitor and coach.

Dr ANNE DE LOOY: Anne is head of Dietetics and Nutrition at Queen Margaret College, Edinburgh, and tutor to the National Coaching Foundation on sports nutrition.

Dr PETER THOMAS: Peter is a sports physician in Reading and was an Olympic oarsman in the Mexico Games of 1968. He was then the Great Britain rowing team doctor and is currently the medical director of Reading Sports Injury Clinic and a medical officer at the British Olympic Association's Medical Centre at Northwick Park.

ROB YOUNGS: Rob is a senior lecturer in Physical Education, Sport and Leisure at De Montfort University, Bedford. He is a former English Volleyball Association staff coach and past chairman of the EVA technical commission. As well as having tutored for the National Coaching Foundation, Rob has taught volleyball courses at the Blackpool Easter school and the Loughborough summer school.

Introduction

Volleyball is one of the most popular team sports in the world and is played by sunbathers for 5 minutes a year up to dedicated international players contesting Olympic medals. It is a versatile sport – truly a sport for all.

However, despite the spread of the game throughout the world since its invention in 1896, and the recent television coverage given in Britain, it remains less popular here than in many other countries. Nevertheless, there is an enthusiastic following and members of the English Volleyball Association (EVA) in 1994 number over 25,000, compared with just over 10,000 in 1984.

People play sport for many different reasons, ranging from health and fitness, social enjoyment and relaxation to competition and skill development. For whatever reason they may give, most players want to improve their game by becoming more skilful, improving their physical fitness, being better mentally prepared, or perhaps for other factors. Certainly, *improvement* in one or more aspects of the game is likely to underpin continued involvement in volleyball for many players (particularly young players). Part of the satisfaction in playing a sport like volleyball is the personal enjoyment from playing as well as you can and, certainly for competitive players, from *preparing* well for the matches.

These days success in sport is usually only achieved through a well-planned and executed *training programme*. Adherence to such a programme (at whatever level) is, of course, likely to lead to personal improvement and greater satisfaction. The purpose of this book is to guide you through the principles of training for volleyball. But, this is done with a difference! Most sports books concentrate on the *skills* of playing the game – understandable, given their importance. However, (because of limitations of space) very few give much information on the different aspects of training. Only passing reference is made in these books to circuit training, weight training or a 'mental approach'. Accordingly, this book aims to provide you with a more complete picture of the training process, including:

(i)   volleyball practices
(ii)   physical fitness
(iii)   nutrition
(iv)   injury prevention
(v)   mental training

This thorough approach is recommended as the best way of preparing yourself for the game of volleyball.

1 Individual and Group Practices

Volleyball is a team sport that can cater for everyone – male or female, élite performer or total novice, handicapped or able-bodied, age six or sixty. This flexible game can be conditioned in many ways to suit the abilities of the participants. It can be played in the gymnasium, sports hall, park, or on the beach.

This chapter gives a series of progressive practices, covering all of the basic skills of the game, which can be done singly, in pairs, in threes or in larger groups. Expensive equipment is not necessary and many of the exercises can be done at home or in the playground using a cheap lightweight ball, a length of rope and a smooth wall. These practices are designed to meet the needs of players of all levels and will be of value, not only to those learning the game but also to established club members and coaches.

One of the delights of volleyball is that every player needs to be competent in all of the basic skills, for the rules dictate that participants rotate to play in all six court positions. In the early stages there is no attempt at specialisation, hence all players need to be able to volley, dig, serve, smash, block and move well around the court. This chapter concentrates on these basic skills and contains major coaching points on each one.

THE VOLLEY PASS

Individual Practices

(1) Standing close to the wall, practise throwing and catching the ball, aiming for a point on the wall approximately three metres above the ground. Catch the ball in the

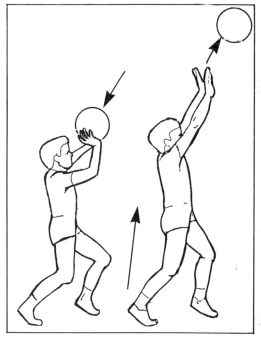

Drill 1

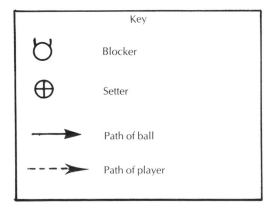

Key	
♉	Blocker
⊕	Setter
→	Path of ball
- - →	Path of player

volley position in front of the forehead with fingers spread and feet staggered; the ball is held momentarily in this position and then thrown against the wall, pushing your arms right out and driving from your back leg. The action should be a spring flexion of all joints as you give on receiving the ball, and an extension of all joints as you make the pass.

(2)   Once you are familiar with the action, reduce the time the ball remains in your hands. Then practise releasing the ball at different speeds and angles so that you need to move to your left or right, or backwards or forwards so that you still catch the ball just in front of and above your forehead.

(3)   Feed the ball to yourself and volley against the wall. Once you are familiar with this, progress to receiving the rebound from the wall with a volley above your head, then volley back against the wall.

(4)   Continuous volleying against the wall.

Once you are confident, you can progress to continuous volleying whilst sidestepping, so progressing along the wall.

(5)   Volley the ball continuously above your head – first set a target of five, then ten, then twenty.

(6)   Volley the ball above your head ten times, sending the ball progressively higher the first five times, then progressively lower for the last five.

(7)   If you are a more advanced player and particularly if you specialise as a setter, stand facing the wall, 'self-feed' and volley against the wall; then receive the rebound with a volley above your head, turn the body 180 degrees whilst the ball is in the air and reverse volley the ball back to the wall.

(8)   This last practice can be a continuous practice; volley to self, turn, reverse volley against the wall, turn, volley rebound to self, turn and so on.

Drill 4

Drill 5

Practice in pairs – one ball

(9)   Facing your partner (about two metres apart) volley the ball high into the air; your partner allows it to bounce once, then volleys it high back to you. Before volleying, allow the ball to bounce; this practice continues as volley – bounce – volley – bounce etc.

(10)   Face your partner, about two or three metres apart. Feed the ball with an underarm toss for your partner to volley back. This can be repeated six, ten or twenty times and then the roles reversed.

(11)   As for the previous practice, but the ball is fed alternately short and long for your partner to move one to one and a half metres forward to volley the ball back to you, and then to retreat to receive the next long feed. This can continue as a predictable alternate feed six or ten times, then progress

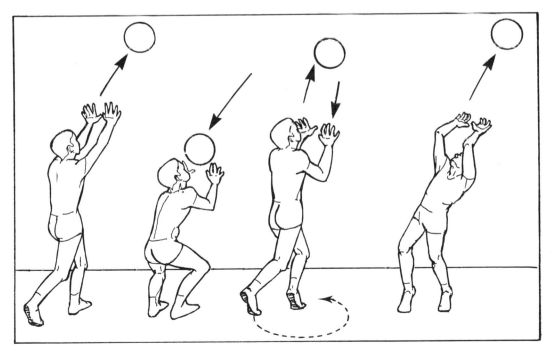

Drill 7

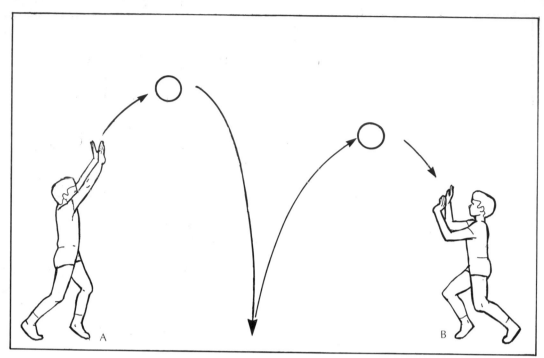

Drill 9

Drill 11(a)

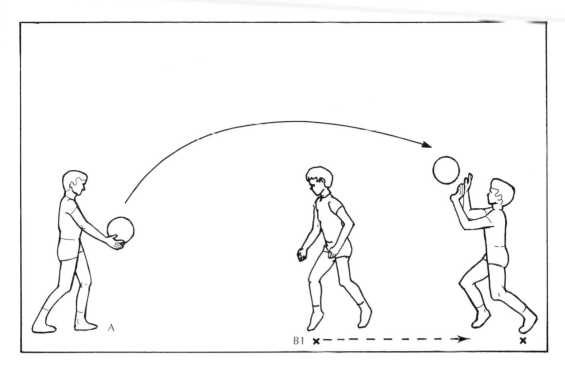

Drill 11(b)

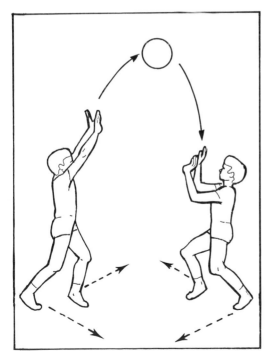

Drill 12

to random feeds with your partner returning to the game starting line each time. (Feeds must be high enough to give the volleyer time to get in position before the ball arrives.)

(12)   Facing each other, volley the ball back and forth continuously. This can be made more challenging by setting a target number of volleys to be achieved; once you have become competent then the practice can include sending the ball to one or other side of the receiving player, making you or your partner move into position before the ball arrives.

(13)   Face your partner, volley the ball to yourself, turn 180 degrees and reverse volley the ball to your partner, who receives with a volley to him or herself and repeats the manoeuvre.

(14)   Stand on the set-shot line facing a basketball backboard and ring; your partner stands beneath the board and feeds the ball with a sympathetic underarm lob for you to volley the ball into the ring. The feeding player retrieves each shot. This practice can

13

be made competitive by giving each player a set number of attempts, scoring three points for a basket, two for a direct hit on the ring that does not go into the basket, and one for a hit on the backboard. The winner could perhaps be the first player to accumulate twenty points.

(15) A one against one conditioned game, played over the net using a small court approximately six metres by two. You are allowed to volley, or play the ball once, twice, or three times before passing it over the net, but may win only a maximum of three points in a row before letting your partner serve. Service is by self-feed and volley over the net.

Drill 14

Practice in Threes – one ball

(16) Stand in a triangle, each player approximately two metres from the others. Feed to the player on your left, who turns and volleys to the third player, who catches the ball and feeds to you, who volley to the player on your left, who catches, and so on.

(17) This practice can progress to a continuous volleying practice around the triangle, changing direction after fifteen passes.

(18) You (A) and one other player (B) act as static feeders, the third player (C) volleys and sidesteps. You feed the ball to C, who turns to volley the ball to B, who catches the ball as player C sidesteps across to line up in front of B. Player B feeds the ball to C, who volleys it back to you. Repeat ten times and then change roles. This can be made more demanding if the feeding player receives the pass with a volley to him or herself and then feeds with a volley, rather than catching and throwing.

(19) Stand in a line, as illustrated. You (player A) volley to B, who returns ball to A. You then make a long pass to C, as the middle player (B) turns 180 degrees to face C. The sequence then becomes: C to B; B

Drill 16

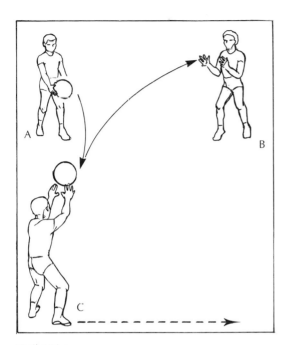

Drill 18(a)

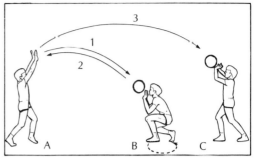

Drill 19

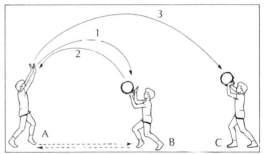

Drill 20

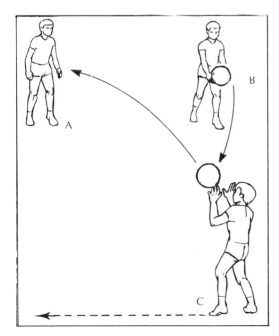

Drill 18(b)

back to C; C over the top to A. After six to ten sequences, the central player is changed.

(20)   As for the previous practice, but as the long third pass in the sequence is made, the player making that pass switches position with the central player. The sequence thus becomes: A to B; B back to A; A to C (players A and B switch positions). The next sequence is: C to A; A back to C; C to B as players C and A switch positions.

(21)   For more able players and for specialist setters the last practice can be adapted so that the central player makes an overhead (or reverse) volley. The sequence now becomes: A to B; B overhead to C (as players A and B switch). Initially the outside players may need to volley to themselves to allow time for the switching to be carried out, but once the practice is running smoothly, the movement should become a single continuous volley for all three players.

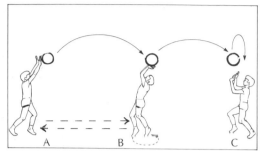

Drill 21

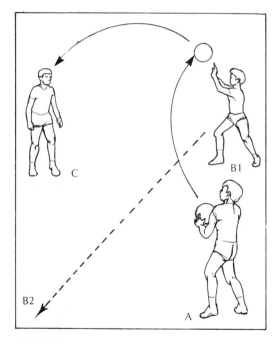

Drill 22(a)

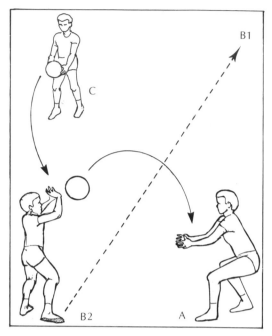

Drill 22(b)

continues with player B running from corner to corner after each pass ten or twenty times, then the working player is changed. This can be a physically demanding practice and to give the moving player time to get into position before the ball arrives, it may be necessary for the outside players to volley once to themselves before passing the ball on.

(23) Players B and C stand three to four metres apart. You (A) start behind C and with the ball. A volleys to B and then runs around behind B. B passes the ball to C, who volleys it to A. Player A returns the ball to C and runs behind C. C passes to B who passes again to A. Thus A makes one volley and then runs three or four metres each time. Having made ten passes, change the running player.

(22) Players fill three corners of a three-metre square – two of the players will remain static, the middle player will be active. You (A) volley or throw feed the ball to B, who turns and volleys to C. Having passed the ball, B runs to fill the empty corner of the square. Player C passes the ball to B who turns and passes to A, then quickly returns across the square to the starting point. This

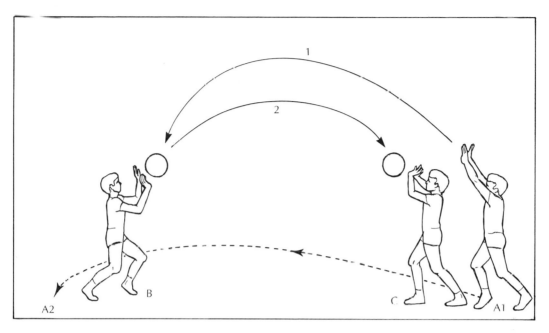

Drill 23(a)

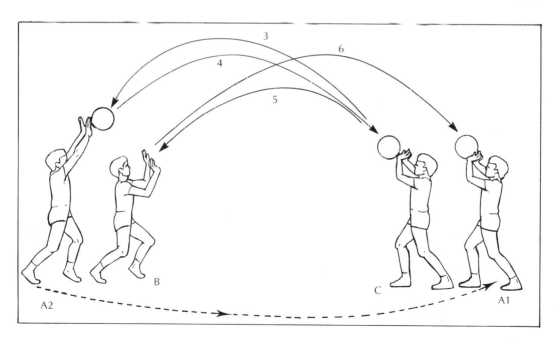

Drill 23(b)

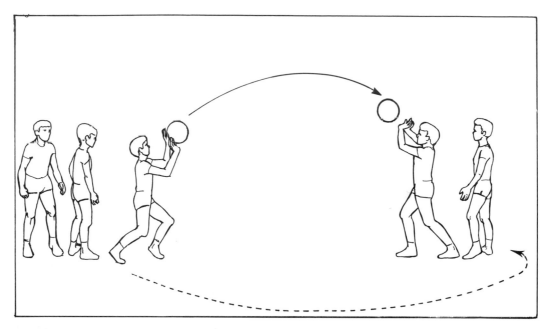

Drill 24

Larger Group Practices

(24)   Groups of two or three facing each other, approximately three metres apart. The front player of one group volleys the ball to the front player of the opposite group and then runs to join the back of the opposite line and so on. This is more demanding in groups of three, but can be done as a practice for groups of four, five, or six.

(25)   The previous practice can be adapted as a setting practice and performed at the net using two lines of players as illustrated. Having volleyed the ball the player moves to join the back of his or her own line. After everyone has made ten passes, the practice can be repeated with players moving to join the back of the opposite line.

(26)   Groups of four, five or six players pass the ball continuously, with the shout of 'mine'. By using the volley pass only, the intention is to keep the ball in the air for as long as possible and also to encourage players

Drill 25(a)

Drill 25(b)

to claim the ball with the call of 'mine'. If a player does not call before playing the ball, or if the ball is played so that no one else in the group has a chance of getting to it to continue the rally, the culprit in each case drops out of the game to do six to ten extra volleys against the wall, or above his or her own head (so two or more balls need to be available). Having completed the extra practice, the player rejoins the group.

(27) This practice, suitably called 'zigzag', can cater for between six and twenty-six players. Feeders are positioned in two lines approximately three metres apart as illustrated. The volleyers move along the lines of feeders and complete two, three or four circuits, depending upon the size of the group. Once familiar with the practice, the feeders can also volley the ball (but may need to play it once to themselves before feeding, to allow the moving player to get in position).

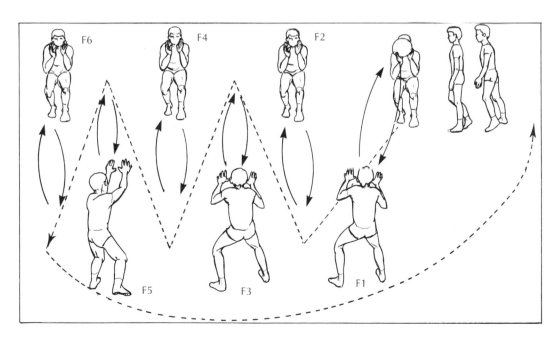

Drill 27

MAJOR COACHING POINTS FOR THE VOLLEY PASS

(i)   Move to get into position before the ball arrives.

(ii)   Turn to face the target before playing the ball.

(iii)   Receive the ball in front of and above the forehead.

(iv)   Position the hands so they are cup-shaped and moulded to the shape of the ball.

(v)   Spread the fingers wide, cock the wrists and thumbs back. Wrists and fingers should be flexible.

(vi)   Elbows should be wide and flexed to receive the pass.

(vii)   Knees should be bent with feet staggered front and back to receive the pass.

(viii) Arms and legs should be extended as the ball is played.

(ix)   The hands and arms should follow through long after the pass is made.

(x)   Give plenty of height to the pass – this is essential and initially more important than accuracy.

Drill 28

THE DIG PASS

Individual Practices

(28)   Stand about two metres from the wall and practice dig passes, allowing the ball to bounce once after rebounding from the wall – so it becomes; dig – bounce – dig – bounce etc.

(29)   As the previous practice but with no bounce. This can be made more demanding by selecting a target on the wall and aiming to dig the ball on to this target area each time.

(30)   Throw the ball against the wall and dig the rebound so that the ball has a high trajectory and drops on to a target area (e.g. mat, or chalked zone) positioned in front of the wall.

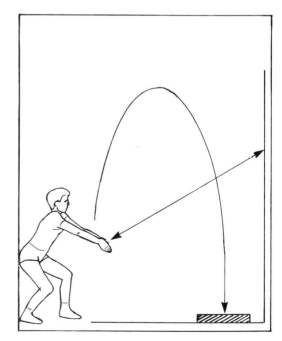

Drill 30

Practices in Pairs – one ball

(31)   Stand three metres from your partner and throw the ball from above your head in a downward trajectory for player B to dig the ball back. After ten passes reverse the roles. This can be made competitive by scoring a point for each time you are able to catch the ball in the volley position.

(32)   Stand three metres from your partner, and dig the ball to each other continuously, allowing one bounce between each pass; dig – bounce – dig – bounce etc.

(33)   This last practice can progress to continuous digging (with no bounce between), setting a target number to be reached.

(34)   Stand three metres apart – one of you will be the feeder who is static and the other one the digger who will move to play the ball. The feeder indicates which side the ball will be fed and gives his or her partner time to move sideways to dig the ball back. After ten dig passes on alternating sides the players change roles. This can be made more demanding if the digger is given less time to get into position before feeding, or if the ball is fed at random, so that the receiver will have to return to a mid-point, not knowing which side the next ball will be fed.

(35)   Feed the ball with a downward trajectory volley pass for your partner to return with a high dig pass. This is performed as a continuous passing practice with the players

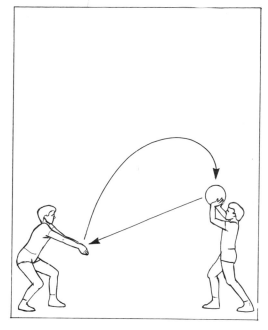

Drill 31

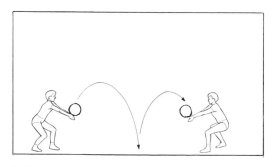

Drill 32

Drill 34

changing roles after twenty consecutive passes. With experienced players this can be made more demanding if the volley feed is played in front of, or to one side, of the dig player, so making him or her move to get into a new position to receive the ball.

(36) Stand with your back to the wall, defending a goal two or three metres wide. Your partner – the shooter – can only score with a volley from about two metres, which must be aimed below your shoulder height and you can only save the shot with a dig action. Each player is given ten shots – or remain in their role until three goals are scored. The size of the goal can be modified according to the abilities of the players, and if they are experienced, the shot can be by soft smash, rather than volley.

Practices in Threes

(37) Form a triangle, each player two metres apart. Throw the ball low for the second player (B) to turn and dig to C, who catches. Player C then feeds you (A) who dig to B who catches. Player B then feeds C, and so on. This can be developed to continuous digging around the triangle, changing direction after twelve passes.

(38) The previous practice can be developed, from the sequence of feed, dig, catch, to volley, dig, volley, dig, etc. around the triangle – the volley pass being low and the dig pass high.

(39) This practice involves one static feeder facing two players who dig and then run to touch a mark two or three metres away before returning to dig again. As the feeder, you should feed – either with a low thrown ball or with a volley pass – player B, who digs the ball back to you (A) and then runs, returning to take up position behind C. Change roles after twenty passes.

(40) Two players – about three metres apart – are feeders with a ball each. Player C stands facing feeder A, receives the thrown

Drill 37

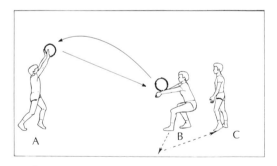

Drill 39

feed, and digs back to A. The digging player C then runs to face feeder B, digs the feed ball back to him or her and returns to face A to repeat. This is a pressure practice and player C can be made to work harder by feeders releasing the ball earlier, or by being further apart. After twenty dig passes the moving player is replaced. If experienced, the feeding players can volley to themselves and then feed with a volley pass.

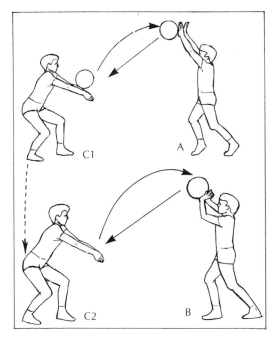

Drill 40

(41) Stand facing a basketball ring, while the second player (B) stands beneath the basket, and the third player (C) stands at right angles with the ball. Player C feeds the ball low for you (A) to turn and attempt to dig the ball into the basket. Player B retrieves the ball and returns to C. After ten scoring attempts, the players rotate one position. One point is scored for a ball hitting the backboard, two for a direct hit on the ring which does not go in and three for a basket.

Larger Group Practices

(42) This is a practice for four or five players and requires three players to form a triangle (players A, B and C) with the extra player(s) standing behind A, who holds the ball. A passes to B and then follows the ball to take up B's position, B digs to C and follows the ball, C digs the ball to player who started behind A. Thus it becomes a

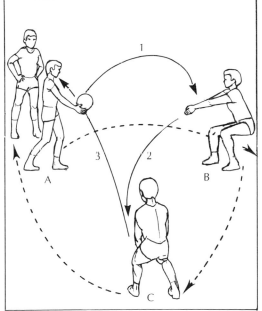

Drill 41

Drill 42

continuous digging drill around a triangle, the players moving on one position with each pass.

(43)   Feeders stand with their backs to the net with a ball each. Opposite each feeder is a digger, positioned just inside the base line. The ball is thrown from high to low (to simulate the smash or service) for the digger to return high to the feeder. The digging player then moves on one position clockwise to receive the next ball. Having played all the balls on one side of the net the digger then moves round to the other half court and completes the same exercise there. Each digging player does three circuits of the court and then takes the place of a feeder. This practice can cater for as few as six players using half the court or up to twenty or more on a full court.

(44)   One player, close to the net at zone 2, feeds the ball towards two or three players who are positioned in the back court, low and ready to dig the ball to a target player at the net. Spare players are used as retrievers to keep the feeder supplied with balls. After a set number of feeds each player moves on one position.

(45)   For more experienced players or for a variation of this practice, the feed can be in the form of a soft smash.

(46)   The feeder stands at the net with a supply of volleyballs and a target player (or catcher) next to him or her. Other players form two lines behind the base line and there are two retrievers off court. At a signal from the feeder, the player at the front of line A comes on court, shuffles along the base line, takes up a deep, low position and is fed the ball to dig back to the catcher. The digging player then goes to the back of line B and the front player from B comes on court, shuffles to the opposite corner, is fed the ball to dig and then joins the back of line A etc. After a set number of feeds, the target player, retrievers and feeder take the place of the diggers.

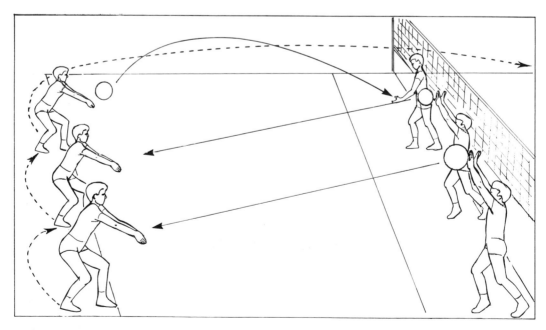

Drill 43

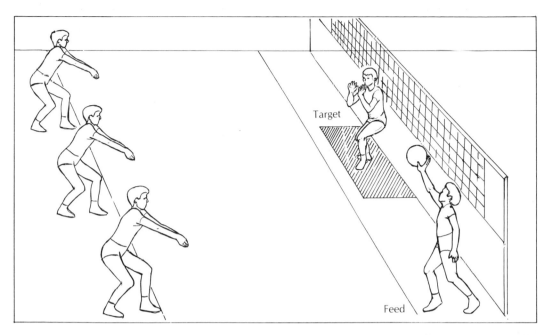

Drill 44

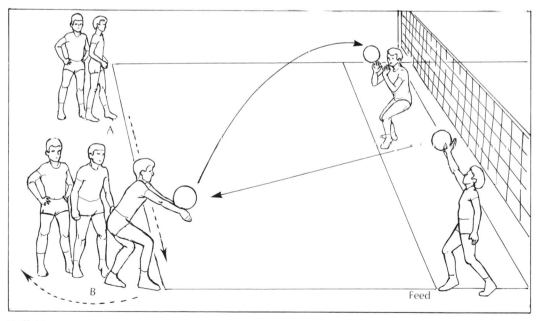

Drill 46

MAJOR COACHING POINTS FOR THE DIG PASS

(i)   Do not interlock the fingers and keep the thumbs parallel.
(ii)   Lock the elbows by extending the arms and wrists.
(iii) Play the ball on the forearm between the wrist and elbow.
(iv)   Bend the knees to receive with the feet staggered front and back.
(v)   Place the outside foot forward and turn the body to face the target before playing the ball.
(iv)   Drive up and through with the legs, keeping the shoulder movement to a minimum.
(vii) Do not swing the arms at the ball: keep the platform stable.
(viii) Relax the upper body and pass the ball high.

THE SERVICE

Individual Practices

(47)   Stand facing a wall, serving to hit the wall above a line of bricks or markings equivalent to the height of the volleyball net. You should work to become confident and consistent with your technique, slowly moving backwards, eventually reaching a point nine metres from the wall.
(48)   As in the previous practice, but with target zones marked on the wall to aim at.
(49)   Stand behind the base line of the volleyball court, within the service zone, with a supply of volleyballs. Targets are placed on the court in the form of mats, chairs or skittles for you to serve over the net and hit.
(50)   If there is no volleyball court, but gymnastic equipment is available, you can use climbing ropes, practicing your serve between them. (For each of these practices

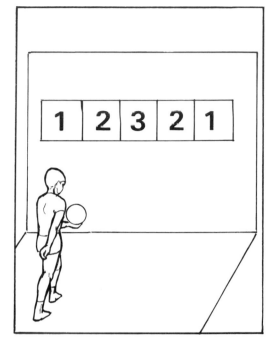

Drill 48

motivation is increased if a second player acts firstly as a retriever and then as a competitor.)

Practices in Pairs – one ball

(51)   Face your partner, standing on either side of the net approximately six metres apart. Serve in turn, aiming for your partner, who catches the ball and serves back. If the ball is caught without the receiver having to move more than one step then the serve has been successful and the server takes a step backwards for the next service. Thus both players are trying to work towards their base line, but if you are unsuccessful with your service, you remain where you are.
(52)   Your partner takes up a position on court beyond the net to receive your service with a catch. Take turns at serving and being targets – each time the positioning of the target should change.

(53) Face each other either side of the net, the server behind the base line, the target player some two metres in court. If the ball is caught by the target player without having to move, then three points are scored by the server, if one step in any direction is necessary then two points and if two steps, only one point is scored. Take turns at serving and the competition can be either the first to reach twenty points or who can gain the most points from ten serves each.

Practices in Threes

(54) Stand with a ball behind the base line, from where you will serve; player B stands just beyond the net holding up a large hoop for you to aim at; player C acts as a retriever, and returns the ball to the server. After ten serves the players all change position.

(55) Stand with a ball behind the base line, from where you will serve; player B stands in the opposing court as a target; player C stands at the net in B's court. You serve for B to dig pass the ball to C, who catches in the setting position and returns to you. After ten serves each player rotates one position.

(56) Similar to the previous practice but developed for more experienced players, the sequence now being serve, dig, set, smash. Player A serves, player B digs the ball to C who now sets the ball for B to smash over the net back to server A. After ten sequences each player rotates one position.

Larger Group Practices

(57) Two teams of players stand behind their respective base lines. The first player in each line serves from within the service zone to a target player in the opponents' court. This target player catches the ball and keeps the score of the number of serves caught. Having caught the ball he throws it behind

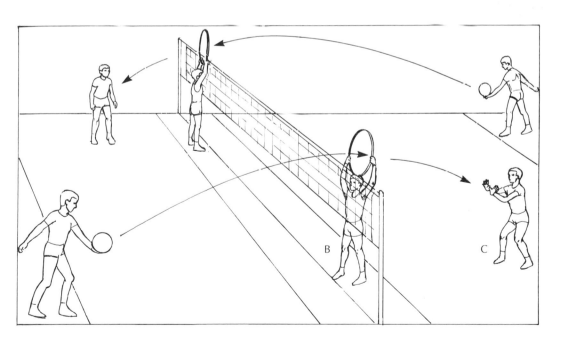

Drill 54

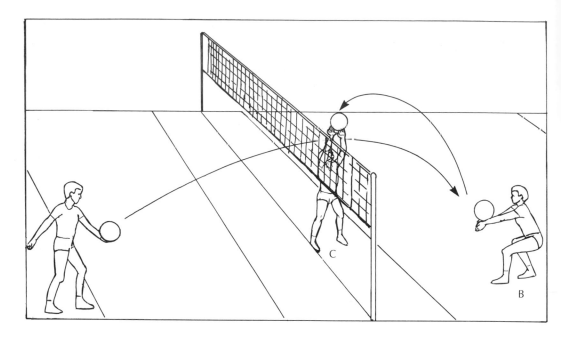

Drill 55

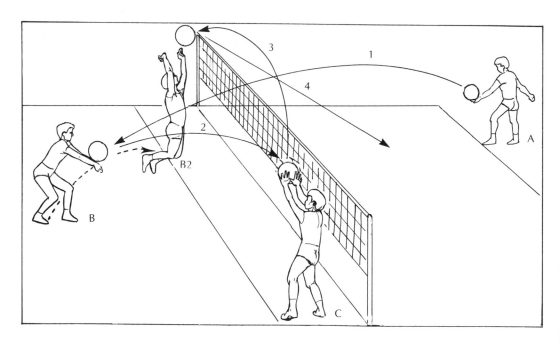

Drill 56

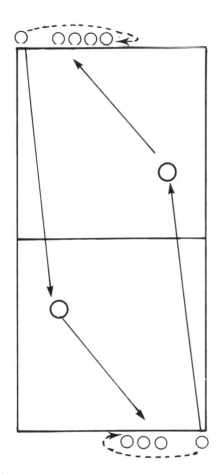

Drill 57

MAJOR COACHING POINTS FOR THE SERVICE

(i)   Ensure the feet are behind the base line.
(ii)   Release the ball from the hand before serving.
(iii)   Have the feet staggered, with the foot on the other side of the body from the hitting hand at the front.
(iv)   Bend the knees, transfer body-weight from the back to front foot.
(v)   Keep the hitting hand firm.
(vi)   Line the feet up on target.
(vii)   Ensure controlled and consistent release of the ball.
(viii)   Take time and care over service.
(ix)   Get on to the court quickly once the ball is in play.

THE SMASH

Individual Practices

(59)   Stand facing a wall, about two metres away, and hold the volleyball in your non-hitting hand at shoulder height. The ball is hit into the ground to rebound off the wall and be caught again. You can develop this practice by tossing the ball higher so that you jump up and smash the ball.
(60)   As the previous practice, but continue to hit smashes into the floor from rebounds off the wall without catching the ball.

Practices in Pairs

(61)   Stand facing a wall, about three metres away, with your partner standing alongside, ready to feed you the ball. He or she, using a two-handed underarm toss (for accuracy), feeds you the ball in front of your hitting arm for you to jump and smash the ball into the ground. Change roles after six to ten feeds.
(62)   As the previous practice but start further back from the wall, so that you

for the other serving team to use, and, after each player has served, he or she moves to the back of his or her own line to await another turn. This team competition can be highly motivating for young players and is also good preparation for club players since the coach can decide upon a particular target zone for service practice.
(58)   If fewer players than are required for the above practice are available, it can be modified so that the target is a mat, chair, cones or skittles placed instead of a catching player. As in the previous practice, the target can be moved after a set number of serves or after a certain time-limit is reached.

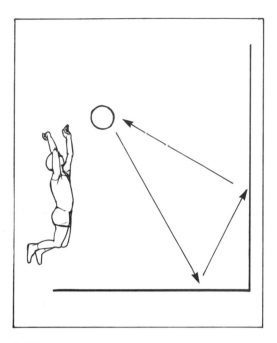

Drill 60

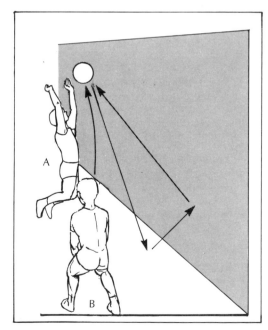

Drill 61

approach with a two or three-step pattern followed by a jump with both feet, again hitting the ball into the floor in front of the wall.

(63) Start on the three-metre line with a ball, and with your partner at the net. Throw the ball to your partner, who, with an underarm toss, feeds for you to approach, jump and smash the ball over the net at a target area on the far court. After six to ten smashes the players change position.

(64) As the previous practice, but throw the ball in high for your partner at the net to feed with a volley. Again a target area should be used and players should reverse roles after six to ten attempts.

Practices in Threes

(65) The previous two practices may be performed with a third player acting as a retriever behind the target area.

(66) For experienced players a combination practice can be devised, involving serve, dig, set, smash. However, if the emphasis is on improving your smash technique it is important that this practice does not break down through poor performance of the other skills. Serve to player B, who digs the ball to C standing at the net, who in turn sets the ball for player B to approach the net and smash the ball back to you. Rotate one position after six to ten smashes.

(67) Start with the ball three metres back from the net, with player B in the setting position at the net, and player C on the far side of the net positioned mid-court. Toss the ball high to B who sets the ball up for you to approach and smash over the net at C. Player C receives the ball with a dig pass played high to B – who has moved under the net to catch the ball. Players repeat the practice six to ten times and then change roles.

(68) Players adopt the same starting positions, but target player C catches the ball. Setter B moves under the net, is thrown the

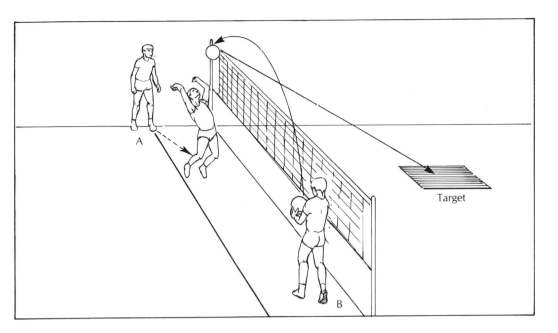

Drill 63

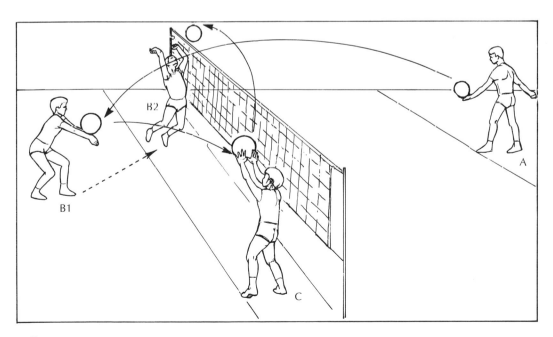

Drill 66

ball by C to set it up for him or her to approach the net and smash over at you (A), (now the target player). Thus players A and C are alternately smashing and being target players whilst the setter B is setting the ball up for each hitter in turn.

Larger Group Practices

(69)   This practice involves a line of players who approach and smash from zone 4 on the court, and a line of feeders with a ball each at zone 3 (see Glossary). The front player in zone 3 feeds the ball for the first hitter to smash at a target area on the court. This practice can cater for a large group (if less than eight, only one half of the court is used), and for such groups the whole court is used, with players moving on from being the feeder at zone 3 to join their own hitting line at zone 4; and from hitting at zone 4 to collecting the 'smashed' ball and joining the opposite feeding line.

(70)   The previous practice can be developed so that the targets are players who then dig the ball to the player at the back of the feeding line at zone 3. If teams set the ball from zone 2, then the practice can be modified so that there is a catcher at zone 2 on the receivers' side of the net. The rotation thus becomes: feed, smash, under the net to catch, dig receive, feed, smash, etc. (See also Drill 87.)

(71)   Both of the last two practices (69) and (70) can be carried out using a volley to set the ball up, but again care must be taken to ensure that the practice does not break down through the poor standard of volleying. If a team uses specialist setters, these players should be used extensively in practices as the feeders. During practice, mention should also be made of the necessity to approach the net at the correct angle, depending upon whether the smasher is left or right-handed. If the hitter is right-handed he or she approaches the net at zone 4 from a wide

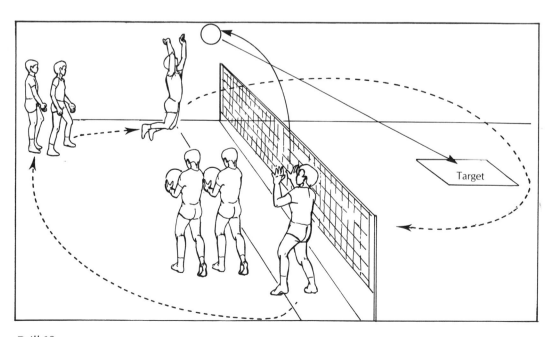

Drill 69

angle, starting off court for a conventional high set, but from zone 2 the approach is in a straight line parallel to the side-lines. For left-handed hitters the opposite applies.

MAJOR COACHING POINTS FOR THE SMASH

(i)   Approach the net from approximately three metres away.
(ii)   Wait until the ball is at maximum height before starting the approach for a conventional high set.
(iii)   Take a long last stride, lower the body, line up hitting arm.
(iv)   Rock back on the heels at the end of approach.
(v)   Take off from two feet.
(vi)   Make a vigorous upward swing of both arms at take-off.
(vii)   Keep the shoulders square to the net.
(viii)   Ensure the hitting arm is pulled back, and the arm is bow-shaped with the elbow leading.
(ix)   The wrist should be cocked and the hand open.
(x)   Hit the ball at maximum reach height in front of hitting shoulder.
(xi)   The hitting hand caps the ball and then the wrist (which must be flexible) follows through.
(xii)   Do not touch the net.
(xiii)   Aim for placement rather than power.
(xiv)   Vary the angle of approach, from zone 4 and zone 2.

THE BLOCK

Individual Practices

(72)   Jump up, simulating a blocking action, to touch a mark on a wall, at the net, a branch on a tree or some other suitable site. Repeat six to ten times, rest and repeat again.

Drill 74

(73)   Practise any bounding or hopping action to develop local muscular endurance in your legs. Activities such as squat jumps over a bench or elasticated rope, 'giant striding' or step-ups will help increase leg power and enable a blocking player to jump higher. (*See Chapter 2.*)

Practices in Pairs

(74)   Stand opposite your partner on either side of and close to the net. On the count of three both you and your partner jump up to reach over the net and clap hands.
(75)   As in the previous practice, but on landing you both sidestep in the same direction for two steps and then jump to block and touch hands again.
(76)   Stand opposite your partner on either side of and close to the net. Hold a volleyball two-handed above your head and on the count of three both of you jump up, your

Drill 76

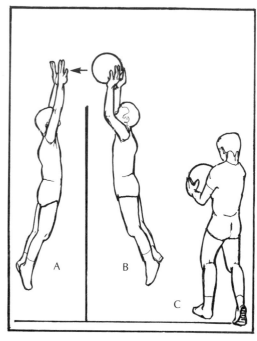

Drill 77

partner reaching over the net to take the ball from you. This can be repeated five, ten or fifteen times.

Practices in Threes

(77) Stand at the net, ready to block. The other two players (B and C) alternately run in towards the net from the opposite court – to simulate the approach of a smasher – jump up and throw the ball into the blocker's hands. The angle of the approach by B and C can be varied, as can the distance back from the net from where they jump, so giving the blocker practice at moving along the net to 'line up' the block and practise the timing of the block jump.

(78) A similar practice to the previous exercise involves one approach player jumping up to throw the ball into the hands of two players blocking together. The players at the net should 'separate' after each block, since

Drill 79

an important aspect of the practice is to make the players familiar with coming together to form a good composite block. After six to ten blocks the players change positions.

(79) Three players perform a set-smash-block drill. Start three metres from the net and throw the ball high to player B, who is at the net in the setting position. B sets the ball up with a volley for you to approach and soft smash the ball for player C to block. After ten attacks the players rotate positions. (The emphasis remains on improving the block technique, so care must be taken that the practice does not break down because either the set or the smash is poor.)

Larger Group Practices

(80) A row of three to six players stands on benches at the net, each holding a volleyball at stretch-height above the net. The rest of the group will sidestep along the length of the net and jump to block against each ball (which must be held very firmly by the players on the benches). The blocking players can be asked to repeat the practice two, three or four times, and the exercise can be made progressively more difficult if the order of players holding the ball begins with the shortest and ends at the far end of the net with the tallest, so making the blocking player jump successively higher.

(81) This practice involves a line of blockers at zone 2 and zone 3 on one side of the net and a line of feeding players at zone 4 on the opposing side. The front player at zone 4 approaches the net and jumps to throw the ball into the block (the two blockers having come together with the outside lead blocker

Drill 80

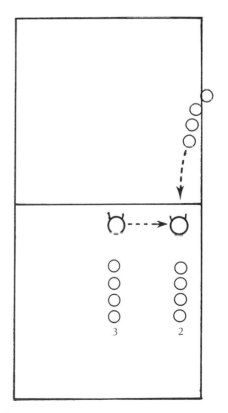

Drill 82

35

determining the line and timing of the block). After each block the players move to the end of their respective lines and after a series of twenty blocks the players in the line at zone 2 move to zone 3, those who were in zone 3 move to the other side of the net to become attackers, and those who were feeders at zone 4 move under the net to block at zone 2. Thus the rotation is from lead blocker, to inside blocker, to attacker.

(82) For variation with an average size group or if the group is large, this practice can be performed using both sides of the net.

(83) Drill 81 can be adapted by having a setter at zone 3 in the attackers' court. The ball is thrown to the setter by the first attacker – set back, parallel to the net, at zone 4 for the attacker to come in and jump

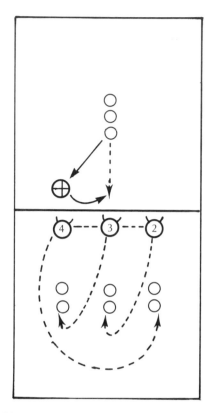

Drill 86

volley the ball into the block. After each block the lead blocker joins the back of the inside blocking line and the inside blocker joins the back of the lead blocker's line.

(84) This can be developed to include a soft smash instead of a jump volley, but again it must be remembered that the emphasis is here on block improvement rather than smash.

(85) The previous practices can be repeated with the blocking lines at zones 4 and 3, the attack coming from the opposition's zone 2.

(86) If the standard of volleyball being played results in the opposition attacking through zone 3, the previous exercise may be adapted so that there are three blockers at the net. Lines of players ready to block stand

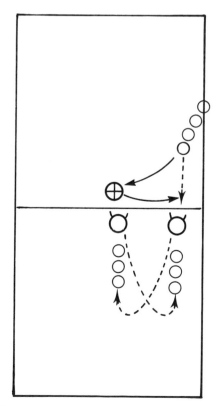

Drill 83

in zones 2, 3 and 4, while on the other side of the net is a line of attackers at zone 3 and a setter at zone 2. As the attack comes through the middle – by thrown feed, jump volley or smash – the two outside blockers move in towards the central blocker who lines up and sets the timing of the block. After three attacks the blocking players rotate – number 2 joining the back of line 3, number 3 joining the back of line 4, and number 4 joining the back of line 2.

MAJOR COACHING POINTS FOR THE BLOCK

(i)   Side-step along in front of the net (crossover technique may be favoured by more experienced players).

(ii)   Hold hands at shoulder height, elbows in to the side.

(iii)   Line up the block with the smasher's hitting shoulder.

(iv)   As lead blocker do not watch the ball, but watch the hitter's approach path.

(v)   Jump vertically off both feet from a half squat.

(vi)   Take off just after the smasher for a conventional high set – the further back he or she is from the net, the later the block goes up.

(vii)   Reach over the net with the hands.

(viii)   Make your hands cup-shaped with fingers spread wide.

(ix)   Angle the outside hand so that it deflects the ball into play.

(x)   Avoid touching the net.

(xi)   With a two person block, the outside player sets the block.

COMBINATION PRACTICES

For more able and experienced players practices can be devised which combine a number of the basic skills to form game-

related situations. Two such practices are described below.

(87) This practice involves the skills of service, dig pass, volley, smash, block and 'back-court-smash reception' – and is built up as a progressive practice in five stages. Players first of all are positioned in the service zones with a ball each. The target player B (or digger) is positioned at a deep zone 4 and a further player is off court waiting to replace the digger. At the net at zone 3 player C waits to catch the ball in a

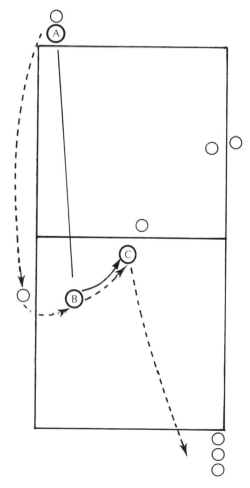

Drill 87

volley position. The sequence of passes is: A serves to B; B digs to C; C catches and takes the ball back to join the serving line. The players rotate one position, so that the server becomes the off-court digger, who in turn becomes the on-court digger, the digger the catcher and the catcher the server.

(88)   The practice then progresses to serve, dig, set, smash, with players rotating as before. Player A serves to B; B digs to C; C sets to B; B smashes over the net.

(89)   The third phase is for the server to remain deep on court and then become a target player receiving the smash with a dig

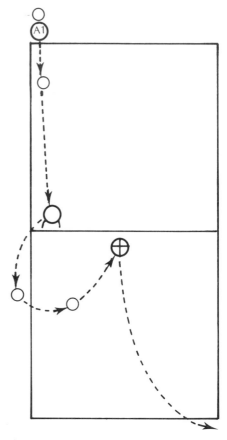

Drill 90

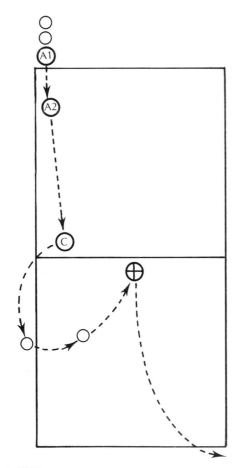

Drill 89

pass and playing the ball to a catcher at the net. The rotation now becomes: server, catcher at net, waiting digger, digger/smasher, setter, server.

(90)   The fourth progression includes the block so that the practice becomes: serve (and stay deep to receive any ball that beats the block); block, but once the ball is past, turn to catch the ball from the back-court digger, wait to dig, dig/smash, set, move on to serve.

(91)   The final phase increases the number of blockers to two (and with a large group of players includes a close covering player behind the block). The rotation then becomes:

(1) serve (and back court target player), (2) covering player (behind the blocker), (3) inside blocker, (4) outside blocker, (5) waiting digger, (6) digger/smasher, (7) setter, (8) server.

(92) The second combination practice is as follows: players are positioned on either side of the court as; a line of smashers in zone 4, a setter in zone 3 and a lead blocker in zone 2. The setters are worked constantly throughout this practice, alternating between setting and blocking. The first hitter on side A throws the ball to setter A who sets for the hitter to come in and smash. The setter on side B side-steps across to join the lead blocker and once the ball is either blocked (or passes the block) the setter on side B reverts to the setting role. At the same time

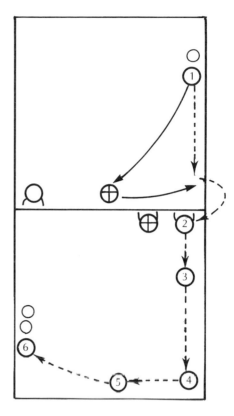

Drill 93

the setter on side A side-steps across to join the lead blocker. Thus each side attacks in turn as the setters switch from setting to blocking. The hitter rotates to become lead blocker on the opposite side of the net, and the lead blocker joins the hitting line on his or her side of the net.

(93) The previous practice can be developed to include covering positions behind the block, so that the rotation of positions becomes: (1) smasher, (2) lead blocker, (3) close cover (behind blocker), (4) deep cover behind blocker at zone 1, (5) deep cover behind blocker at zone 5, (6) join new hitting line.

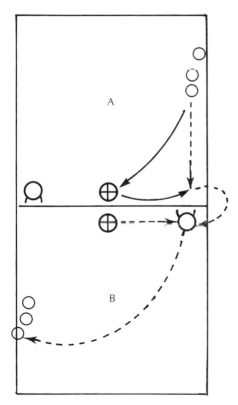

Drill 92

SMALL-SIDED CONDITIONED GAMES

Small-sided games are an essential part of coaching young players in volleyball and can also be of great value in the training sessions of even the most experienced players. Situations of one against one, two against two, three against three and four against four can all be managed in many ways in order to develop particular aspects of the game or specific skills. Various conditions can be imposed, such as players only being allowed to volley, insisting upon three-touch on service reception or requiring the setter to play every second pass. Indeed, it may be that three-touch volleyball is obligatory at all times throughout the rally. The great value of small-sided games is that players touch the ball far more frequently than in the conventional six against six situation and so skill acquisition is improved. Of course, the ability of the players will very much determine the nature of the conditions imposed upon the practice session.

MOVEMENT PRACTICES

The following practices are designed to encourage players to get in position well before the ball arrives. Volleyball is an active game and all players have roles to fill and positions to move to as every ball is set.

(94)   Two against one. Using a small-sided court, player A starts with the ball and serves over the net to player B, who passes to his setter, player C. C sets to B and having done so ducks under the net to become the setter for player A.

(95)   As for the previous practice, but as the ball is played over the net so the players change roles and the sequence is as follows: A serves to B; B passes to setter C; C sets for B; B plays the ball over the net to A and moves under the net to become A's setter,

while player C retreats to the back of the court. Player A then passes to setter B, who sets for A, who in turn plays the ball over the net to C and moves under the net to become C's setter, while B retreats to the back of the court. Player C then passes to setter A, A sets to C, C plays the ball over the net to B and so on. Thus each player sets the ball, moves to the back of the court, receives the opponents' ball and becomes an attacker, plays the ball over the net and follows it to become a setter on the opponents' court.

(96)   Three against three. On a half-size court two groups of three face each other. The objective of the practice is for three-touch volleyball to be sustained while players are continually moving to cover their

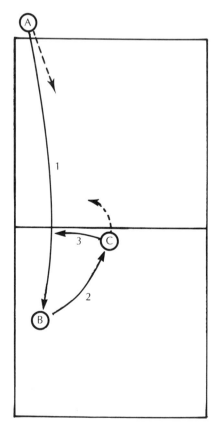

Drill 94

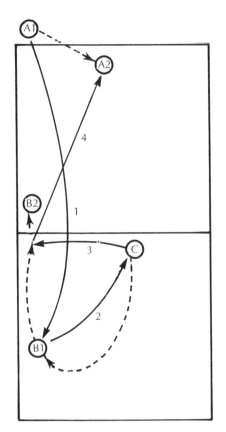

Drill 95

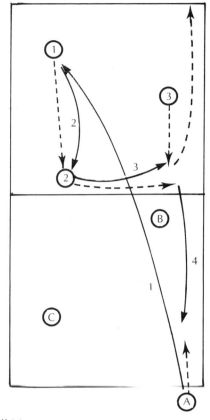

Drill 96

pass. Player A serves the ball for the opposing number 1 to receive. Player 1 passes the ball to setter, number 2, and runs to touch him or her with two hands below the knee. Player number 2 sets the ball for number 3 and runs to touch him/her below the knee with two hands. Player number 3 plays the ball over the net to the opposing player A, positioned in zone 1 and then runs to touch his or her own base line. Player A passes to (and touches) setter B, who passes to (and touches) C, who plays over the net to number 1 and runs to touch base line and so on. After a number of passing sequences the players on each side rotate one position.

(97) Three against three, quick change. Teams of three are drawn up and the full

court is used. The team playing in court A are the 'superstars'; they must play three-touch volleyball and win the rally in order to stay on court and win a point. Other teams are positioned behind the base line at team B's end and try to depose team A either by winning the rally or by preventing team A from playing three-touch volleyball. Service is always with team B and, if succesful, they quickly move under the net to become the new team A, whilst the deposed team A join the back of the line of teams waiting to come on as servers at team B's end.

(98) Six against six. Team A serve and adopt the conventional six against six service formation, whilst Team B stand on the attack line. On the first whistle receiving team B

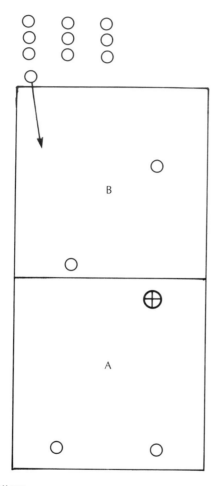

Drill 97

move to adopt their reception formation and on the second whistle the player in zone 1 on team A serves. The rally is played out and each player is given three to ten serves. With every new server the receiving team – before the whistle is blown – first stand on the centre line, then on the base line, the side

lines, and finally divided so that some players are on one line and some on another. In this practice the quality of the first pass is often considerably improved as players are awake, in position and set before the ball arrives; as players become familiar with the practice so the delay between the two whistles can be reduced.

(99) Six against six – 'sit as ball crosses net'. As the title implies, each time the team plays the ball over the net, including service, the six players must sit on the floor and then quickly get back to their feet to continue the rally. This is a physical conditioning practice and can become quite demanding. The aim is to keep the rally going as long as possible using only underarm service, volley and dig pass.

(100) Six against six – 'front and back court switch'. As in the previous practice there is no attempt to win points here but to sustain a lengthy rally. Every time the ball crosses the net the team that hit the ball switches their front and back court players. Each time the rally breaks down both sides rotate their players one position.

CONCLUSION

Having practised the skills of volleying, digging, serving, smashing and blocking and having combined them into multi-purpose practices and worked to improve movement on court, the reader should now be well prepared to play volleyball to a much higher standard. Continued practice will lead to improved performance and increased enjoyment.

2 Physical Fitness

The constant rise in standards in sport can be attributed to many things, such as improved techniques and equipment. What heights, for example, would pole-vaulters be managing without fibre-glass poles? However, in some sports the equipment is relatively unimportant and the techniques may not have changed much. What, then, can account for improvement in such sports? Quite probably, the key factor is physical fitness. Not only does it contribute to the end result (to whatever extent) in volleyball, but it is now recognised that fitness is a very important part of training. Indeed fitness is important at all levels of the game because while it is essential for international competition, it is also beneficial for beginners, improving both their effectiveness and their enjoyment of the game.

WHAT IS PHYSICAL FITNESS?

Physical fitness involves a multitude of components, so making it difficult to identify fitness as one single thing. In fact, when people ask how fit you are, they are asking a rather naive question. If I was asked the same type of question about my car, I might reply that it is excellent for comfort and good on motorways, but not good for acceleration and in need of improvement when starting in the wet! An overall comment on how good (fit) my car is depends upon which aspect you are referring to.

Similarly, we can refer to many different parts, or components, of fitness. Nowadays there is a great deal of interest in fitness for health, which includes exercises for stamina (e.g. jogging), posture, weight control etc.

However, fitness for sport will include some of these components as well as others, such as speed and power. The importance of each component for your sport obviously depends upon the sport itself. Volleyball is a dynamic 'all-round' game which requires most types of fitness. Nevertheless, you can imagine the marathon runner and weight-lifter having – for the most part – quite different fitness training programmes.

The components of physical fitness for sport which require physical training are summarised in Fig 1. Many years ago sports coaches used to refer to the main components of fitness as the 'six Ss' – stamina, strength, speed, suppleness, skill and (p)sychology! One could easily add diet and nutrition, injury prevention and other areas to Fig 1. However, the diagram refers to the main components of fitness which require physical activity and changes in the physiological state of the body.

A final point on the definition of fitness; it is sometimes claimed that fitness is a set of attributes that individuals have or achieve and which help in the ability to perform physical activity. The phrase 'have or achieve' is interesting since it suggests that

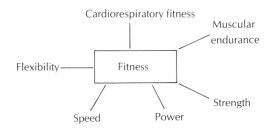

Fig 1 A model of physical fitness-training components for sport.

sporting fitness is dependent upon two things: natural ability ('have') and training ('achieve'). Many aspects of fitness are governed by our heredity, yet with training we are able to make the most of what we have. Unfortunately, 750cc Fiats will never race in Formula One events. However, you might enjoy racing a good 750cc Fiat if it is given the right care and attention, especially if you compete against cars of the same type. Indeed, with good maintenance (training) the 750cc Fiat will be able to beat a less well maintained car with a larger engine.

PRINCIPLES OF FITNESS TRAINING

Regardless of the fitness component we are talking about, certain basic principles apply to all aspects of fitness training in sport. These are:

- frequency
- intensity
- progressive overload
- time
- type (of exercise)
- specificity
- reversibility

Frequency

Frequency refers to the number of training sessions during a particular time period. It is usual to speak of frequency in terms of sessions in a week. Most sports require two or three sessions per week, although obviously those people striving for the highest honours will train much more frequently. (Indeed, many sports today require their top athletes to train several times a day!) However, for most people, significant fitness improvements can be made with about three sessions per week.

Intensity

This refers to how hard one should train. This will differ greatly between individuals although similar training programmes can be performed on a relative basis. This means, for example, that two athletes can perform three sets of five repetitions of the leg-press exercise in the weight-training room at 75 per cent of their maximum. However, the actual weight lifted may differ considerably. Superior athletes with an extensive training background are also likely to be able to train at a higher level for longer and to recover more quickly. The intensity of the training will largely determine its effectiveness. Too little intensity will not produce much of an effect, while too much is likely to lead to injury and fatigue. For these reasons, the principle of progressive overload is important (see Fig 2).

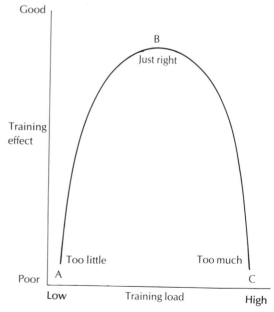

Note A→B effect of progressive overload

Fig 2 Progressive overload.

Progressive Overload

The old story of Milo carrying a calf on his shoulders is the perfect illustration of progressive overload. Milo started off carrying a small calf, but as the animal grew in size and weight, Milo did not find it progressively more difficult to carry. Instead, he adapted to the increasing load as his muscles grew stronger. Eventually, he could carry a fully-grown bull. Two things are important here: first, Milo was *progressive* in his 'training'. He gradually adapted to the increasing load. Imagine what would have happened if he had tried to lift the bull having had several months of inactivity! Second, Milo adapted to the load through *overload*. This is a fundamental mechanism, since with training, the body will grow and adapt to increased work (with sensible progressive overload) or collapse (through inappropriate training – too much too soon). This is illustrated in Fig 2.

Time

This simply refers to the amount of time spent in a training session. This will vary greatly depending upon the sport and the individual. Most fitness training sessions, allowing for adequate warm-up and cool-down, last upwards of 40 minutes.

Type (of Exercise)

Fitness training sessions will vary in terms of the type of exercises used. Some sessions will contain predominantly cardiorespiratory exercises, others strength and flexibility, and so on. This will depend, again, on the individual and the sport in question.

You may have noticed that the above concepts can be easily remembered by using the word FITT, the letters standing for frequency, intensity (including overload), time and type. This 'FITT principle' forms the corner-stone for many sports' fitness training programmes. However, there are other basic principles to remember.

Specificity

Ultimately the aim of your fitness training must be to make you a better volleyball player. It may be very satisfying to improve your time over your favourite three-mile run, but if it doesn't help your volleyball it is misplaced effort. Fitness training, therefore, should be specific to the sport in question. However, this does not mean that the fundamental components of fitness are ignored. It would be pointless to train for hours every day to improve your finger strength for setting, when you lack the fundamental agility and speed to get into position to be an effective setter! A combination of exercises is therefore required.

Reversibility

'Use it or lose it!' is a common expression in sport. Unless you continue training, the fitness you have built up will quickly be lost. Some people seem to retain their fitness better than others, but these individuals probably have a high natural ability to perform, as mentioned earlier. They will still lose the benefits of training if they fail to continue, but the effects may not appear so marked. A run-down Formula One car will still beat a well-tuned 750cc Fiat!

COMPONENTS OF FITNESS FOR VOLLEYBALL

Volleyball is a fast game requiring players to develop all the qualities outlined in Fig 1. However, in volleyball, some of these components are more important than others. Fig 3 gives a guide to the relative importance of each of the fitness components for

Fitness components	Not very important	Useful	Important	Very important
Cardiorespiratory fitness		●		
Muscular endurance			●	
Strength			●	
Power				●
Speed (and agility)				●
Flexibility			●	

Fig 3 Fitness components for volleyball.

volleyball. The purpose of this section of the chapter, therefore, is to outline each of these components and show how they can be developed to maximise their effectiveness in volleyball. Before these components are dealt with in turn, it is important to say something about the warm-up.

Warm-Up

An important part of the training process, the warm-up is a period of exercise performed prior to the main part of the training session or competition. It is used to prepare the body for more vigorous action later. The warm-up can be divided into two main phases: general warm-up and sport-specific warm-up.

The general warm-up should consist of two main exercises: gentle, rhythmic, 'total body' exercises, such as jogging or calisthenics, which should slowly increase in intensity and produce a slight sweat and raised pulse and secondly static stretching exercises (see section on flexibility later in this chapter).

The sport-specific part of the warm-up, as the name suggests, should include exercises which specifically prepare you for your game, such as jumping exercises for spiking, wrist and finger stretches for setting etc.

These can then be followed by practices of the skills themselves. The warm-up process for volleyball is summarised in Fig 4.

In addition to preparing to start activity, you should also prepare to finish! This is done by cooling-down after periods of vigorous activity, using similar exercises to those in the warm-up, such as gentle rhythmic exercises and stretching. In fact, this is a particularly good time for stretching as your muscles will be warm and so very receptive to this form of exercise.

CARDIORESPIRATORY FITNESS

Let us first try to understand the terminology! Cardiorespiratory (CR) fitness can also be known as cardiovascular fitness, aerobic exercise, stamina fitness, and probably a host of other names. Sports scientists may not always agree on the correct term, but for our purposes cardiorespiratory fitness is probably good enough. It is the stamina-type fitness associated with cycling, jogging and swimming. The local muscular endurance fitness needed in exercises like sit-ups or press-ups is, of course, very much related to cardiorespiratory fitness, since it is the CR system that

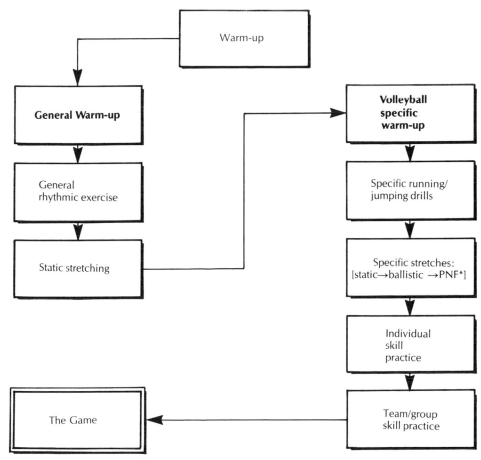

see flexibility section of this chapter

Fig 4 The warm-up process for volleyball.

is responsible for getting oxygen to the working muscles. However, specific local muscular endurance will be considered separately since a whole set of different exercises can be prescribed for this fitness component.

Physiologists have long known that the body operates through different types of 'energy system'. For example, the weight-lifter and shot-putter require short bursts of high-intensity effort, whereas the marathon runner needs prolonged effort at a lower intensity. The three main energy systems are summarised in Fig 5. From this table you will see that CR fitness, or stamina, is associated with the 'aerobic' energy system. The word aerobic means 'with air' (or oxygen) and refers to continuous activities whereby the oxygen that is breathed in is sufficient to supply the energy required for that particular activity. Hence walking is aerobic and sprinting is 'anaerobic' (without oxygen/air) as high-speed sprinting cannot be sustained for long (*see* Fig 5). Anaerobic training will be considered later in this chapter.

	ENERGY SYSTEMS		
	1	**2**	**3**
Duration	0–15 secs	15secs–2mins	Over 2mins
Technical term	ATP–PC system	LA (lactic acid)	Aerobic system
Description	Strength, power, speed	Short-term muscular endurance	Long-term muscular endurance and aerobic activity
Volleyball activities	Spike, block	Rally	Very long rally, recovery between plays

Note: ATP=Adenosine triphosphate
       PC =Phosphocreatine

Fig 5 The main energy systems of the body and their practical meaning in volleyball.

Aerobic Endurance

Aerobic CR fitness is developed by progressively taxing the CR system (i.e. heart, lungs, blood vessels, blood) and so the most practical indication of aerobic training intensity is heart rate, or pulse. It is generally thought that gains in CR fitness will occur when the heart rate (HR) is raised to a sufficient level for a 'training effect'. But what is a sufficient level? As a general rule optimal gains in CR fitness occur when the HR is raised to within 60–90 per cent of maximum, where maximum is estimated as 220 minus your age (in years). This figure gives the number of beats per minute. For example:

Person: A. Robic
Age: 20 years
Estimated maximum HR:
220–20   = 200 beats per minute (bpm)
Training zone = 60–90% of max.
              =120–180 bpm

This is likely to yield a conservative estimate at the lower end of the range for most active sportspeople, so another simpler, method is to add 25 to your age and subtract the sum from 220.

Person: A. Robic
Age: 20 years
CR training intensity
= 220 − (20+25)
= 220 − 45
= 175 bpm

You can count your own pulse either at your wrist or your neck. At the wrist (the radial pulse) simply place three fingers (not your thumb) lightly on your upturned wrist at the base of the thumb. It is probably easier to count for fifteen seconds and then multiply by four for your bpm figure. Errors will occur but these should diminish with practice. A stronger pulse can be felt at the neck (the carotid pulse) by placing the fingers gently against the neck at the base of the angle of the jaw bone. For reasons of safety, do not press too hard.

Fig 6 summarises the FITT principle for aerobic fitness training. This shows minimum criteria and many active sportspeople will require greater levels of training.

FITT Component	Minimum criteria
Frequency	3 times per week
Intensity	Elevated heart rate 60–90% of maximum, or 220 – (age + 25) beats per minute
Time	20 mins
Type (of exercise)	Gross body exercise, such as running, swimming, cycling

Fig 6 The FITT principle as applied to cardiorespiratory training.

Moreover, for maximum benefit in the game of volleyball the types of exercise used should be as relevant and similar to volleyball as possible. This suggests that swimming and cycling will not be as effective for the volleyball player as running, and that running might best be done in 'interval' form to simulate the stop–start action of the game itself.

However, it is important to remember that the CR system is central to recovery from all forms of exercise, so although volleyball players need not have the running endurance of the long-distance athlete, they do need a fundamental base of adequate aerobic fitness. Fig 7 shows how a volleyball player might develop aerobic fitness on court by using interval training. Numerous variations on this theme are, of course, possible and the coach should vary such practices a great deal.

At times, and particularly with more advanced players, volleyball skills practices can be mixed in with these fitness routines. This can be useful for several reasons:

(i)   it provides a form of training similar to the actual game
(ii)   players can immediately see the point of the activity
(iii) it allows for variety in fitness training

However, caution needs to be exercised

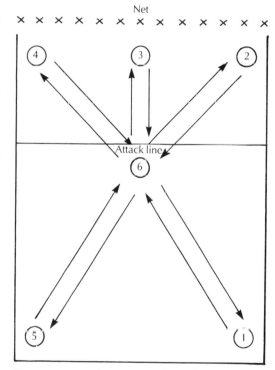

Note: start at 6 and return to 6 at the end of each run; try six circuits, with equal time for exercise and rest periods.

Fig 7 Aerobic training using the volleyball court.

since the load placed on the player should not be so great that the skills are performed badly; fatigue is a major cause of skill breakdown – so beware.

Term	Definition
Strength	The maximum force that a muscle, or group of muscles, can generate. Sometimes the statement 'at a specified speed or velocity' can be added to this definition because force will diminish as the speed of the limb increases.
Muscular endurance	The ability of the muscle, or muscle group, to continue applying force.
Power	The product of force and velocity. In simpler terms strength × speed.
Flexibility	Range of motion about a joint or series of joints.

Fig 8 Definition of terms applied to muscle fitness.

Assessing Aerobic Fitness

The best way to use fitness tests is to compare scores over time for the same player. In other words, use tests to track progress. Simple field tests can be used, such as recording the distance run around a track in twelve minutes, the time taken to run one and a half miles and so on. Assuming that the conditions (including the motivation of the athlete) stay the same from one test to the next, changes in scores give some indication of changing fitness levels. Another simple indication is to step up and down on a bench or stair approximately 50 cm high (although the exact height does not greatly matter). Perform for a set time (perhaps five minutes) to a definite rhythm or beat and then take your pulse. If this exercise is repeated at a later date in exactly the same way any change in the pulse will give some indication of CR fitness changes. Such simple methods can be appealing but are only rough guides to progress. With the growing availability of laboratory testing, more accurate measures should be possible for a greater number of players.

In concluding this section on aerobic fitness, you should remember that volleyball is primarily an anaerobic game requiring power, agility, and speed more than high levels of aerobic fitness. Nevertheless, vol-leyball does require adequate aerobic fitness and this should be developed early in the training cycle, although greater increases in performance are likely to occur with an emphasis on strength and speed (power), muscular endurance and flexibility training. These areas of 'muscle fitness' will be considered next, but before proceeding you should check the definitions of these terms in Fig 8.

The different components of muscle fitness listed in Fig 8 are often interrelated. For example, to develop power, both strength and speed are necessary. For the sake of simplicity, however, most areas will be considered separately, but you should bear in mind that the overlap between one area and another area does exist.

MUSCULAR ENDURANCE

This aspect of fitness follows on naturally from aerobic fitness. Since muscular endurance is the ability to repeat muscle contractions over time, such as repetition sit-ups, improving this component of fitness requires relatively high numbers of repetitions to be performed. (This is the reverse of strength development, as explained later and illustrated in Fig 9.) It is clearly the case that large numbers of repetitions can only be performed with a relatively

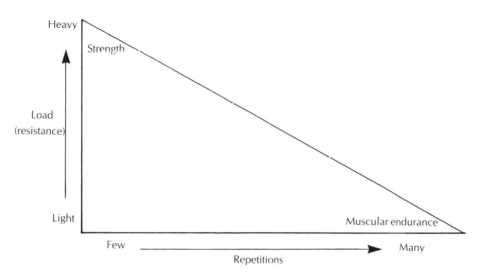

Fig 9 The strength–muscular endurance continuum.

Name	Figure	Muscle action
Press-ups	11 (i)	Back of upper arms (triceps) and chest
Pull-ups	11 (ii)	Front of upper arms (biceps), shoulders and upper back.
Sit-ups	11 (iii)	Stomach
Back extensions	11 (iv)	Back muscles

Note: people sometimes refer to 'pull-ups' as involving an overgrasp grip and 'chins' as an undergrasp grip. The effect is similar. You should always perform sit-ups with bent legs, and for back extensions you should not lift shoulders far above hips.

Fig 10 Basic body-weight muscular endurance exercises.

small resistance. While this could be external resistance, such as weights, it is often sufficient simply to use body-weight, such as in press-ups and sit-ups. A series of basic body-weight endurance exercises is shown in Fig 10 and in Fig 11.

More specific application to volleyball can be made by constant repetition of certain game skills – for example, repetition setting against a wall, repetition digs from a low crouch position and so on. It is possible to increase the difficulty by using a slightly weighted ball. However, care should be taken that the skills are exactly replicated: this is also the case if wrist or ankle weights are used. (These are small packs of weights which can be strapped to either the wrists or ankles to provide added resistance.) Other volleyball-specific exercises are shown in the section on strength development.

(i)

(ii)

(iii)

(iv)

Fig 11 Muscular endurance exercises.
(i) Press-ups.
(ii) Pull-ups.
(iii) Sit-ups.
(iv) Back extensions.

Assessing Muscular Endurance

Basic tests of muscular endurance are simple to perform, although always dependent on the subject performing at maximum effort and motivation. As with the CR tests, you can use them to plot individual progress. Any muscular endurance exercise can be used as a test as long as it can easily be measured — for example, the number of sit-ups performed in a set time. Of course, comparisons are only valid if techniques are always the same.

STRENGTH AND POWER

No other area of physical fitness has suffered more than strength training from misunderstanding and mythology. The 'circus strongman' image still persists in many instances, but it is no easier to find 130kg shot-putters lifting weights than slim 800m runners. Weight-training, the most common of strength-training methods, is simply a way of increasing the resistance placed on the muscles to stimulate their growth and development. While on this subject, some popular misconceptions need correction: women will *not* become masculine if they lift weights; it is *not* possible for muscle to turn into fat; weight-training will *not* slow you down. Indeed modern-day athletes use strength and power training extensively, although some sports are more advanced in their methods than others. In short, every dynamic sport requires some form of resistance training.

Before proceeding, it is worth looking again at Fig 8. Very few sports involve maximum force at slow speeds and most require fast strength (i.e. power). As power is a combination of strength and speed, the latter two terms will be dealt with together, although pure speed will be considered separately.

Without going into great detail on how muscles actually work, it is worth noting briefly that there are different types of muscle fibre. 'Slow-twitch' (ST or type I) fibres, as their name suggests, are endurance fibres with low power. The 'fast-twitch' (FT or type II) fibres are the opposite – powerful but only able to operate briefly.

In fact, there are two subdivisions of type II fibres; type IIa and IIb. The latter has a very fast-twitch action, while type IIa fibres are still fast-twitch, but with some endurance capacity. We all possess both types (ST and FT) of fibre in varying proportions, the ratio being determined by heredity. However, through a process of self-selection it is likely that marathon runners will have a high percentage of ST fibres, and sprinters a high percentage of FT fibres, although within these two extreme groups, great variation probably exists. Fig 12 summarises the differences between the two main types of fibre, and Fig 13 illustrates the order in which the fibres are always recruited.

This order (type I, then IIa, then IIb), and the associated intensity of exercise needed to bring about this recruitment, tells us that heavy resistance training (high loads with repetitions of six or less) may well be the best way to develop explosive strength. This contradicts the commonly held belief that heavy resistance training will slow you down. Once repetitions start to exceed about six, the initial tension on the muscle is reduced and fewer type IIb fibres are recruited. This does not mean, of course, that pure speed training, as outlined later, is of no use. (Indeed it is very important for skill and neuro-muscular reasons, and is likely to assist in the translation of the power and strength development into a more functional form.)

Characteristic	Slow twitch	Fast twitch
Aerobic capacity	High	Low
Anaerobic capacity	Low	High
Contraction time	Slow	Fast
Force	Low	High
Activities	Endurance-type	Sprint/explosive type
Fatigue	Slow	Fast

Fig 12 Summary of characteristics of fast and slow-twitch muscle fibres, adapted from Fox, E.L., Sports Physiology *(Saunders College, 1979).*

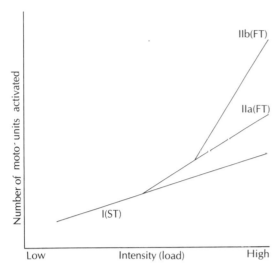

Fig 13 Pattern for recruitment of muscle fibres.

Types of Strength and Power Training Methods

There are several different methods of developing strength. A selection of these are as follows:

(i) Constant resistance (sometimes called isotonic); the conventional type of training involving barbells, dumbells and body-weight. Although called constant resistance, this is slightly inaccurate since the actual resistance on the muscle will change as the body levers create different forces. However, this is probably the most accessible form of effective strength training.

(ii) Static resistance (isometric); force is applied to an immovable object and so no movement is observed. This is not a very useful form of training for sport because of its static nature. It is also unsafe for older people as it creates sharp elevations in blood pressure.

(iii) Same speed training (isokinetic); performed with the aid of a machine which will only allow the limb to move at a set speed. The resistance on the muscle depends on the voluntary effort of the athlete. This form of training has some benefits for water sports, and requires the use of special machines, such as isokinetic swim benches.

(iv) Variable resistance; performed on machines which vary the resistance put on the muscle through its range of movement. This helps overcome the inherent weakness of iso-tonic training whereby the muscle is only working at maximal force in one part of the range of movement. However, variable resist-ance machines are still not readily available to all athletes and tend only to cater for single-joint actions. Since most sports demand actions which are multi-jointed a combina-tion of isotonic and variable resistance exer-cise is desirable.

Exercises can, of course, be differentiated according to the part of the body you wish to develop, i.e. lower, middle or upper. However, in addition to this it is worth split-ting the exercises into three types according to their function; general, specific and competition-specific.

General strength/power exercises are required by almost all sportspeople for basic increases in strength and power in the major muscle groups of the body, such as the legs, back and shoulders. Specific exercises are those which work the muscles particularly relevant to the sport in question, in this case volleyball. Competition-specific are those resistance exercises which copy, as closely as possible, the actual skills needed in the par-ticular sport. For example, one exercise for volleyball players might be repetition block-ing with wrist and ankle weights attached. Figs 14, 15 and 16 suggest some resistance exer-cises for each of these categories. These are then illustrated in Figs 17–32 while Figs 33–35 explain how the exercises should be performed.

Exercise	Major muscles involved	Equipment	Figure
Power clean	Hips, legs, back	Barbell	17
Front squat	Hips, legs (quadriceps)	Barbell	18
Leg extension	Quadriceps	Machine	19
Leg curls	Hamstrings	Machine	20
Side bends	Oblique (side) abdominals	Dumbell	21
Bench press	Chest, triceps, shoulders	Barbell or machine	22
Latissimus pull-down	Latissimus dorsi (side of chest)	Machine or pulley	23

Fig 14 General resistance exercises for volleyball players.

Exercise	Major muscles involved	Equipment	Figure
Split squats	Quadriceps (and for hip flexibility)	Barbell	24
Dumbell bench jumps	Quadriceps, hips, calves	Dumbells and benches	25
Dumbell press	Shoulders, triceps	Dumbells	26
Straight arm pull-over	Chest, side of chest ('lats'), shoulders	Barbell	27
Plyometric exercises	Hips, quadriceps, calves	Benches or gym boxes	28

Fig 15 Specific resistance for volleyball players.

Exercise	Major muscles involved	Simulated skill	Equipment	Figure
Standing block jumps	Quadriceps, hips, arms	Blocking and jumping	Dumbells	29
T-bench lateral rotation	Forearms, triceps	End of spike	Dumbells, bench with 'T' cross-piece	30
Shot catch on trampet or bouncer	Forearms, shoulders	End of spike	Trampet or bouncer, 5kg indoor shot	31
Crouching dumbell press	Triceps, shoulders, quadriceps, hips	Setting	Dumbells	32

Fig 16 Competition-specific resistance exercises for volleyball players.

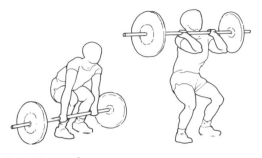

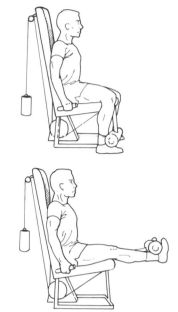

Fig 17 Power clean.

Fig 18 Front squat.

Fig 19 Leg extension.

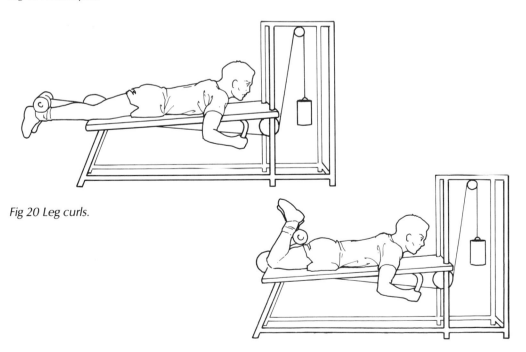

Fig 20 Leg curls.

Fig 21 Side bends.

Fig 24 Split squats.

Fig 22 Bench press.

Fig 25 Dumbell bench jumps.

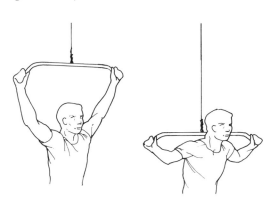

Fig 23 Latissimus pull-down.

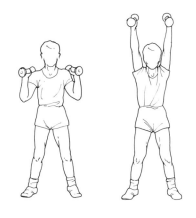

Fig 26 Dumbell press.

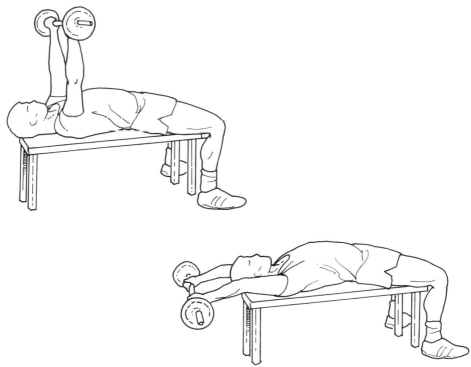

Fig 27 Straight arm pull-over.

Fig 28 Plyometric exercises.

Fig 29 Standing block jumps.

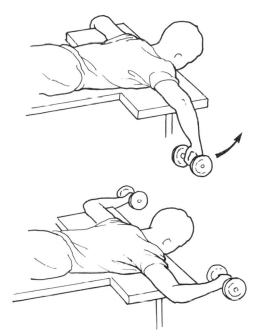

Fig 30 T-bench lateral rotation.

Fig 32 Crouching dumbell press.

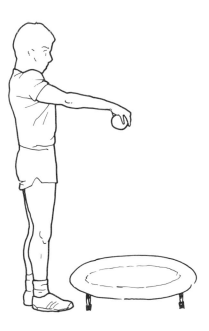

Fig 31 Shot catch on trampet or bouncer.

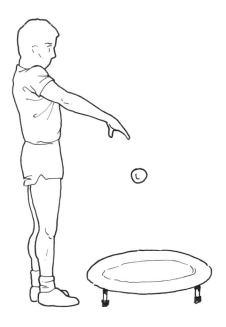

Figure	Exercise	Starting position	Movement	Other points
17	Power clean	Feet under bar, hip-width apart. Shoulder-width overgrasp grip. Hips below shoulders. Arms straight, back flat.	Lift bar from floor with straight arms and keep back flat. Extend body. Keep bar close in. Turn wrists over and receive bar on front of shoulders. Bend legs to receive bar. Lower to thighs, then to floor.	Have bar 20 cm off the floor to start with. Use blocks or wooden disks for this. Make movement smooth and, later, fast and dynamic.
18	Front squat	Bar on chest, high elbows. Feet flat just outside hip-width.	Squat under control to 'thighs parallel'. Return to standing. Keep chest up throughout.	Avoid deep squatting.
19	Leg extension	Feet under lower pads. Sit upright.	Extend legs; lower under control.	
20	Leg curls	Face down on machine, heels under top pads.	Bring heels up towards buttocks. Return under control.	
21	Side bends	Stand with feet beyond hip-width. Dumbell in one hand at the side, other hand behind head or at the side.	Bend sideways with weight, return to middle position and beyond to position of stretch. Return to start.	Move sideways only. Don't use a dumbell in each hand.
22	Bench press	Lie face up on a bench. Hips, shoulders, head all on bench. Shoulder-width grip of bar.	Lower bar to chest. Extend arms until fully straightened.	If using a barbell rather than machine, beginners may find it easier to balance if they start the exercise with the bar on the chest.
23	Latissimus pull-down	Seated or kneeling. Wide overgrasp grip of bar, arms fully extended.	Pull bar down to base of the neck. Return under control.	

Note: although specific breathing techniques can be recommended for each exercise, it is often easier, particularly with beginners, simply to suggest that they breathe freely and naturally. Do *not* hold your breath during the execution of these exercises. This applies to all the exercises in Figs 17–32.

Fig 33 Explanation of general weight-training exercises.

Figure	Exercise	Starting position	Movement	Other points
24	Split squats	Bar on front of shoulders, elbows high. Feet split front and back. Front foot flat, toes pointing slightly inwards. Rear foot on toes, pointing forwards.	Bend front leg and push hips down and forward. Maintain upright trunk. Push back off front leg once thigh is parallel to floor.	Repeat exercise with other foot forwards.
25	Dumbell bench jumps	Place two benches 1.5m apart. Hold a dumbell in each hand at shoulder height.	Jump over each bench without stopping between the jumps.	Practise without weights for balance. If matting is used to absorb shock, ensure it is firm and non-slip.
26	Dumbell press	Seated or standing. Dumbell in each hand at shoulder height.	Extend arms fully. Return under control.	
27	Straight arm pull-over	Lie on bench, face up. Barbell held above chest.	Lower bar to low position behind head. Pull back to starting position.	Try this with an empty bar first, and progress in stages.
28	Plyometric exercises	These are bounding-type exercises with or without boxes for varying the height and depth of jumps.		

Fig 34 Explanation of specific weight-training exercises.

Figure	Exercise	Starting position	Movement	Other points
29	Standing block jumps	Start in the block–jump position with dumbell in each hand at shoulder height.	Jump, extending the arms as high as possible. Cushion the landing.	
30	T-bench lateral rotation	Lie face down on bench, elbows out to the side. Arms bent 90 degrees. Hold dumbell in each hand, palms towards feet.	Rotate arms laterally (hand upwards) keeping arms at right-angles. Lower back to starting position.	'T'extension needed on bench to keep arms in correct position.
31	Shot catch on trampet or bouncer	Stand in front of a trampet or bouncer. Hold indoor shot in hand of extended arm.	Using the wrist only, throw the shot onto the trampet. As shot rebounds, catch it and hold it for 2 seconds.	Keep elbow locked throughout.
32	Crouching dumbell press	Start in the same position as for setting. Dumbell in each hand at shoulder height.	Extend legs and arms. Return under control.	Do not jump off the ground.

Fig 35 Explanation of competition-specific resistance exercises.

Planning Strength and Power Training

You should always remember that strength and power training is merely an aid to improved performance in volleyball. The training should therefore be 'cycled', so that the maximum benefits are derived. This can be a complex matter, but space permits only a brief discussion here. Basically, strength/power training should develop through three phases of the year, starting at the end of the season. After a brief rest from the season, the player should start a basic strength programme. This will mainly constitute exercises from Fig 14. As the season approaches, the training should become more dynamic and power-oriented. Exercises from Fig 15 can now be added, and also, as the new season gets closer, competition-specific exercises. During the season itself, the number of sessions may be reduced (perhaps from three to two per week), as now the aim is power maintenance. This process is shown in Fig 36. Using part of the FITT principle, the following guidelines can be offered to vary the training according to the individual.

(i)   Beginner (with weight-training)
Frequency: 2–3 times per week.
Intensity: low, weights should be light enough to perform 8–10 repetitions (reps), 3 sets each exercise.
Time: initially short (30 mins) but could increase to 45 mins.

(ii)   Intermediate
Frequency: 2–3 times per week.
Intensity: medium, occasionally high. Last few reps should be fairly hard (5 sets of 5 reps).
Time: up to 1 hour.

(iii)   Advanced
Frequency: 3–4 times per week.
Intensity: varied, including *occasional* maximums.
Time: up to 1 hour.

The structure of each session should be:

(i)   Warm-up.
(ii)   General exercises.
(iii)   Specific/competition-specific exercises.
(iv)   Cool-down.

	Preparation phase (out of season)	Pre-competitive phase (pre-season)	Competitive phase (during season)
Emphasis	Strength	Power	Power maintenance
Loading (intensity)	High	High	Medium
Exercises	Mainly general	General plus specific (competition-specific)	Mainly specific and competition-specific
Frequency	2–3 times a week	2–3 times a week	2 times a week
Time (excluding warm-up and cool-down)	45–60 mins	40 mins	30 mins

Note: for the beginner or inexperienced player, the preparation phase should be preceded by a more general aerobic fitness-training programme of several weeks. The basic strength exercises could also be learned and practised during this period.

Fig 36 Developing strength and power across the training year.

Assessing Strength and Power

Assessing strength and power is often recommended by coaches and fitness experts, but the measurement of strength can be a problem, particularly for beginners who are unused to maximum muscular effort. Moreover, this form of exercise may be dangerous for the inexperienced athlete, while some exercises require the learning of considerable skills before the athlete should attempt one repetition at maximum resistance. Although safer forms of strength testing (such as grip-strength tests) exist, they are of limited value in most sports contexts. What is more advantageous is to assess power and, in the case of volleyball, leg power.

Fortunately, assessing leg power is considerably easier although, as with all field tests of fitness, this gives only a rough indication of the fitness component. Two tests in particular are well known; a standing long jump and a standing vertical jump. Volleyball players require vertical jumping ability much more than horizontal leg power, so the vertical-jump test is to be preferred, and is illustrated in Fig 37. It is usual to measure the

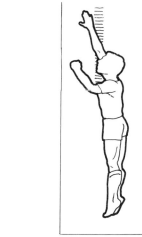

Fig 37 Vertical-jump test.

distance the player can jump above his or her standing reach.

Of course in volleyball it is more important to know who can jump the highest, regardless of their standing height. This can also be determined in order to gauge the likely effectiveness of certain players in, for example, blocking tall players. In addition, the vertical-jump test can be used to assess progress in the resistance-training programme. Improvements in vertical-jump performance should occur after such a programme.

Additional Considerations in Strength and Power Training

Safety

Weight-training has an excellent safety record and particularly so when weight-trainers lift in a well-planned environment with good supervision. Nevertheless, like most activities, a safety code such as the following should be adhered to.

Personal safety
(i)   Learn correct techniques.
(ii)   Train with other people so they can help out if necessary.
(iii)   Warm up properly.
(iv)   Wear appropriate clothing, including training shoes.
(v)   Progress gradually through a planned schedule.

External safety
(i)   Check all apparatus before use.
(ii)   Keep all apparatus well maintained and clean.
(iii)   Have floor space free of obstacles, such as loose disks etc.
(iv)   Plan the floor space for maximum, but safe, use.
(v)   Determine the maximum number of people who can safely use the facility, and then stick to it.

Children

It is tempting, when encouraging youngsters into playing sport, to give them the same training programme as adults. This, however, you should not do, especially when it comes to strength/power exercises. It is generally recommended that pre-pubertal children should not lift weights, although light exercises are unlikely to cause harm. Depending upon the child's development, thirteen or fourteen years is probably the right age at which to start a weight-training programme, in which the emphasis should be on technique and skill learning.

SPEED TRAINING

The volleyball player who has conscientiously trained with resistance exercises (especially the power exercises such as the power clean, Fig 17, or plyometrics, Fig 28) should find that his or her overall movement speed has improved. There are, however, different types of speed in sport. The ability to react quickly to a stimulus is called reaction time and is best illustrated by the reaction of sprinters to the gun. Reaction time can be improved with practice, but only so far. Of course, no one will ever be able to react at the exact same time as the gun.

Equally important in sport is the ability to react *and move* (response time). It is little help to react quickly to the gun if you are a slow runner! It is also important, once the fast movement is under way, to be able to maintain your speed (speed endurance), although this is hardly required in volleyball. Indeed, it is sometimes better in sport to have controlled speed rather than flat out speed, which may create some technical problems. For example, rushing in too fast to block a spike could cause excessive forward motion and an ineffective or illegal block.

Given the strength and power training already outlined, the volleyball player is advised to combine this with speed and agility drills. Here are some examples:

(i) Shuttle running across the court.
(ii) Pressure drills requiring good response time.
(iii) Sprint drills.

A final word on speed training: one further factor which may improve the player's speed of response is experience. This allows the player to become better at reading the game, and so anticipate what will happen next.

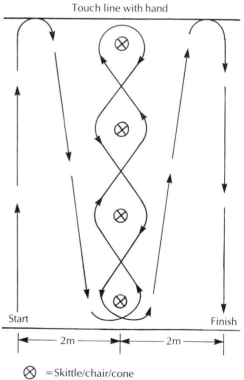

Touch line with hand

Start   Finish

|← 2m →|← 2m →|

⊗ = Skittle/chair/cone

Note: start position is lying face down on floor, with hands by shoulders and head on the start line.

Fig 38 Illinois agility run, reproduced with permission from Adams, J. et al., Foundations of Physical Activity *(Stipes, 1965).*

Assessing Speed and Agility

Assessing sprint speed is relatively easy, although the validity of such measures will depend upon the accuracy of the time-keeper. Moreover, in volleyball, 40m sprint speed is less important than the ability to move fast in an agile way, perhaps to make quick adjustments to retrieve the ball after it is tipped by your blockers. Accordingly, assessment of 'speed' in these situations is actually more a measure of agility – the ability of the player to change body position with speed.

A well-known test of agility is the Illinois agility run, shown in Fig 38. However, since this involves running for over fifteen seconds, a shorter and more dynamic test is more appropriate for volleyball. An example

is given in Fig 39. This is the Nebraska Agility Test and although designed for American footballers, it provides a useful test for volleyball players as well. Of course, there is no reason why volleyball coaches should not devise their own agility test along these lines.

FLEXIBILITY TRAINING

Flexibility – the most neglected area of sports fitness! Certainly this is the case for most sports, with the possible exceptions of gymnastics, swimming and some athletics events, but flexibility is important for several reasons:

(i)   Enhanced flexibility can help in the prevention and rehabilitation of injury.

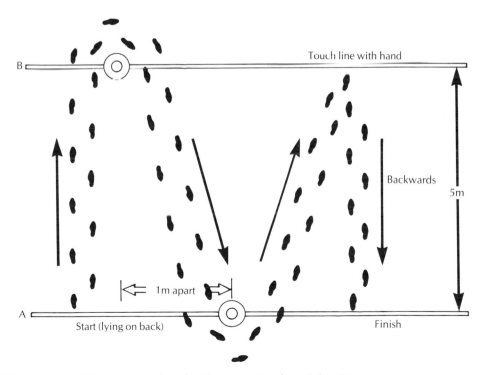

Fig 39 Nebraska agility test, reproduced with permission from Epley, B.,
The Strength of Nebraska *(University of Nebraska, 1980).*

(ii)   Poor flexibility can inhibit the development of some sports skills.

(iii)   Poor flexibility can reduce the effectiveness of other fitness parameters.

To be sure, it is not just for dancers and gymnasts – serious volleyball players need good flexibility too (which really means the range of movement at a joint or joint complex) and so should be spending five or ten minutes each day doing stretching exercises.

Methods of Flexibility Training

There are three main forms of flexibility training; static flexibility, ballistic flexibility and PNF (proprioceptive neuromuscular facilitation!).

Static Flexibility

This method involves stretching a muscle to the point of *mild tension* and then holding it for a length of time in the stretched position. This time can vary but it should not be less than ten seconds. Although some coaches suggest at least thirty seconds (which undoubtedly is effective), this can be boring and may lead to athletes neglecting their flexibility training.

This type of training is a very effective means of improving flexibility and is recommended for all volleyball players. It should always be performed before vigorous activity and before moving on to ballistic flexibility exercises. The best time to improve flexibility is when the muscles are warm, so a good time is often after a game or training. However, you should also practise static stretching before playing volleyball as part of your warm-up (as mentioned at the beginning of this chapter). Athletes should not stretch too much in the belief that 'more must be better'. Stretch to the point of mild tension, not pain! (Fig 40 shows the stretch continuum.)

Partners can be used to help stretch a little further, but you must remember that the athlete stretching is in charge: this is particularly important when groups of children are performing flexibility exercises.

Fig 41 Calf stretch.

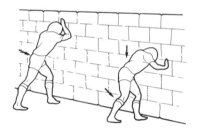

Fig 42 Hamstring and lower back stretch.

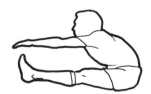

Fig 43 Hip stretch.

Stop here

PREPARATORY STRETCH	DEVELOPMENTAL STRETCH	FORCEFUL OVER-STRETCH
As part of warm-up	To improve flexibility	Too much
To prepare for activity	Best done after vigorous activity	Don't!

Fig 40 The stretch continuum.

Fig 44 Groin stretch.

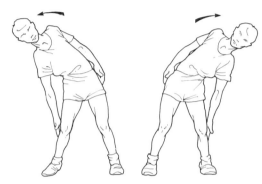

Fig 45 Side stretch.

Fig 46 Shoulder stretch

Fig 47 Wrist stretch.

Fig 48 Arm stretch.

Fig 49 Lying stretch.

Fig 50 Lying shoulder stretch.

Fig 51 Partner shoulder stretch.

Figure	Exercise	Muscles stretched	Starting position
41	Calf stretch	Calf	Lean against wall, foot pointing forwards.
42	Hamstring and lower back stretch	Hamstrings, lower back	Sit on floor, feet together and legs straight.
43	Hip stretch	Front of hip	Lunge position on floor.
44	Groin stretch	Groin, inside thighs	Sit on floor, soles of feet together.
45	Side stretch	Side (oblique) abdominals	Upright stance, feet astride.
46	Shoulder stretch	Shoulders, chest	Standing or seated (legs in front).
47	Wrist stretch	Forearms	Kneel on floor, hands flat.
48	Arm stretch	Shoulder, side of chest	Kneel on all fours, one arm out-stretched.
49	Lying stretch	All-round stretch	Lie face up on floor.

Fig 55 Explanation of static flexibility exercises.

Ballistic Flexibility

A further type of flexibility is ballistic stretching. In this, the muscles are stretched by using bouncing or bobbing movements at the end of the range. There has been some controversy over this type of stretching since it has been indicated as the cause of some injuries. However, while it is never recommended for people on health-related exercise programmes (particularly older people or those with a history of joint injury), it is important and beneficial for sportspeople as most sports require participants to stretch while moving! The obvious example is the hurdler who performs ten ballistic stretches in each race. Ballistic stretching, therefore, is a necessary part of sport, but precautions should be taken to avoid injury. Such precautions include a good warm-up (including static stretches) to prepare the body for more ballistic activity. Care should also be taken that at the end of the range of motion, where the movement is taking place, the bouncing or bobbing is both controlled and gradual. These types of stretches should be specific to the movement required in your sport.

Fig 52 Back lift.

Movement	Other points
(i) To stretch outer calf, keep leg straight and push heel into ground. Push hips forwards. (ii) To stretch inner calf (soleus), bend leg and push forwards and downwards with hip. Keep heel on ground.	Vary position of toes.
Sit up first (chest out) then stretch forwards by reaching towards the toes.	Vary leg positions (e.g. apart).
Push hips forwards.	Progress to more upright trunk position with rear foot on toes.
Gently ease knees outwards and downwards.	Use pressure from arms if necessary.
Bend sideways and hold position.	Avoid leaning forwards.
Lift arms upwards and backwards. Partner lifts arms upwards and backwards, or sideways.	If partner places a knee in the back of the (seated) exerciser, this can help stability.
With fingers pointing towards the body, pull shoulders back to produce stretch on forearms.	Change direction of fingers to alter effect.
Pull shoulder back to produce stretch on top of shoulder, arm and side of chest.	Reach out with hand first.
Extend body position as much as possible.	

PNF Flexibility

PNF is a more advanced and highly effective method of stretching. It involves three basic stages:

(i) Contraction of the muscle to be stretched (for about ten seconds).
(ii) Relaxation of the same muscle.
(iii) Contraction of the antagonist (opposite) muscle, or use of partner assistance.

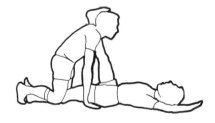

Fig 53 PNF hamstring stretch.

The technique is believed to be effective because the initial muscular contraction allows the muscle to be stretched further. Most of the exercises shown can be adapted for PNF, but you should remember that the muscular contraction will not be effective without something to work against, so apparatus or partner resistance is required. You should use the static method when stretching during PNF. (See Figs 55–57.)

Fig 54 PNF shoulder stretch.

69

Figure	Exercise	Muscles stretched	Starting position	Movement	Other points
50	Lying shoulder stretch with partner	Chest, shoulders	Lie face down.	Partner pulls arms towards mid-line of the body.	
51	Partner shoulder stretch	Chest, shoulders	Partner stands behind you, your arms pointing backwards.	Partners pull arms towards each other.	Pull arms up as well.
52	Back lift	Abdominals	Lie face down, hands behind head.	Partner holds your hands to ease shoulders off the floor.	Avoid excessive back arching.

Note: these need not necessarily be ballistic as each can be performed using the static stretching method. However, they are more specific to volleyball and so may be beneficial if some controlled movement is added at the end.

Fig 56 Explanation of ballistic flexibility exercises.

Figure	Exercise	Muscles stretched	Starting position	Movement	Other points
53	PNF hamstring stretch	Hamstrings	Lie on floor, one leg straight on partner's shoulder.	Push leg down against partner's shoulder (10 secs); relax; partner assists by easing leg back towards head (10 secs).	
54	PNF shoulder stretch	Shoulder, chest	Sit or kneel. Arms out-stretched to the side, parallel to the floor.	Contraction: pull arms forwards against partner resistance (10 secs), then relax. Stretch: partner pulls arms back, keeping them parallel to the floor.	Can also be done with arms above head.

Fig 57 Explanation of PNF flexibility exercises.

Problem Flexibility Exercises

Not all flexibility exercises are necessarily good exercises; when you stretch your muscles, you also put strain on your joints. In most cases, the joints (as well as ligaments and tendons) are being stretched in an acceptable way, but occasionally the joint can be twisted or put under pressure in such a way that could cause injury. Figs 58 and 59 show two of the most common flexibility exercises which should, generally speaking, be avoided.

The ballistic standing toe touch can lead to back problems and should never be performed by people who have had back trouble; it is better for all athletes to use the sit and reach exercise in Fig 42. The hurdler stretch (Fig 59) may lead to problems for those with knee injuries and although this exercise can be effective in improving the flexibility of the hamstrings and groin, it puts a great deal of pressure on the knee joint. Given the likelihood of knee injuries in volleyball (from crouching, diving etc.), this exercise is best avoided.

Developing flexibility, like the other components of fitness, requires planning. Fig 60 summarises the FITT principle as it relates to flexibility training for volleyball players.

Fig 58 Ballistic standing toe touch.

Fig 59 Hurdler stretch.

FITT component	Suggested guidelines
Frequency	Can be done every day, once some experience has been gained. Initially, every other day.
Intensity	To point of 'mild tension' in the stretched muscle.
Time	Each exercise 10–30 secs. Each session 5–15 mins.
Type (of exercise)	Static stretches, followed by PNF and ballistic. Progress from preparatory to developmental stretching.

Fig 60 FITT principle as applied to flexibility exercises.

Assessing Flexibility

Any of the flexibility exercises may be used as tests by simply recording measurements, but two tests of flexibility are particularly recommended. The first is the sit and reach test and is a good indication of flexibility in the hamstrings and lower back – an important part of the body in which to have good flexibility as it can help prevent lower back problems. This test is illustrated in Fig 61.

The second test of flexibility – and one more related to volleyball – is the lying shoulder lift test (Fig 62). Another way to see whether your shoulder flexibility is symmetrical – it is important to have good shoulder flexibility in volleyball – is to try the test in Fig 63. You will probably be better with one hand uppermost than with the other, showing that your shoulder flexibility is not always even; flexibility exercises are useful in remedying this.

Fig 63 Behind back shoulder test.

CHAPTER COOL-DOWN!

After covering the main aspects of physical fitness for volleyball, it is appropriate to cool down before moving on to the next chapter! This cool-down will be a summary of the main points:

(i)   Physical fitness is multidimensional. The main components requiring physical training are: cardiorespiratory fitness, muscular endurance, strength and power, speed and flexibility.
(ii)   Proper planning of fitness training must take into account the frequency, intensity, time and type of exercises (FITT principle), as well as specificity and reversibility.
(iii)   Volleyball players should always warm up before and cool down after training.
(iv)   Volleyball players require a reasonable level of aerobic fitness, but more importantly should be well trained in strength, power, speed and muscular endurance.
(v)   Flexibility is a neglected aspect of fitness and is an important fitness component in volleyball.

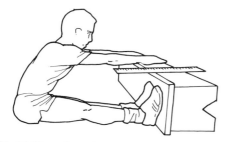

Fig 61 Sit and reach test.

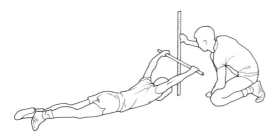

Fig 62 Shoulder lift test.

3 Healthy Eating

Competitors must be well-prepared physically on the day of competition. This preparation, of course, involves many training sessions over the previous months or years. Over this time, food has provided the energy for the competitors to maintain the body and to train. Nutrients in the food – protein, vitamins and minerals – have been used to replenish body losses incurred on a day to day basis. Food is, of course, crucial for the training process.

Food can also be important on psychological and social levels. It may be psychologically important to eat favourite foods or those believed to help performance. For this reason (and probably this reason alone) these foods (often highly peculiar to an individual) are eaten to ensure peak performance is reached and maintained. We all enjoy eating socially with a group of friends and do not want to appear too odd by choosing particularly unusual foods. Accordingly, players may even choose foods which they know are unsuitable. If this happens on an occasional basis it does not matter, but if it is a regular occurrence then it is important to ask why this is the case. It must be emphasised that performance on the day depends primarily on the long period of preceding training (which does include diet).

Eating for your sport can be broken down into two subdivisions; eating for training (which also means for good health), and eating for competition. Both are influenced by who we are, where we are and who we find ourselves with.

REQUIREMENTS FOR FOOD

Eating and drinking is taken for granted by most people. We eat and drink without too much thought and assume that our bodily needs will be met and indeed most of the time they will. However, whether these needs are being met optimally is the question that all serious sportspeople and their coaches should address.

The human body is marvellously resilient, tolerant and versatile. If food-energy intake is less than the body needs the body conserves energy in order to 'balance the books'. People on reducing diets have been observed to be less active and physically slower (so conserving energy) than before embarking on their diet. This has implications for the athlete who is training and deliberately reducing food intake. Is the same effort being put into the training or, indeed, can it? When fed less than they need, young children become less active and grow less quickly as the body attempts to balance its 'energy books'. If a young player is exercising hard, but not able to eat a sufficient amount, it is likely that growth and/or the rate of exercise will suffer. It is not possible to get energy out if insufficient is consumed.

However, there comes a point when the body can no longer adapt to an insufficient intake of food-energy and functions begin to deteriorate very noticeably. Body tissues are not repaired efficiently (they may be broken down and not replaced at all), levels of activity become poor and general health often deteriorates with increased likelihood of infection. Professional medical investigation and treatment may be essential at this point.

The body thus has an adaptive capability and a deficiency response. At the other end of the spectrum (and much more likely to occur in western countries) the body reacts to excessive food-energy intake. Food consumption above requirement will not raise the level of activity or turn individuals into super-performers, although it will encourage rapid growth – in children upwards, and in adults outwards! Eating more protein than the body needs or can use simply results in the excess being excreted. The same is true of water-soluble vitamins such as vitamin C and some minerals such as sodium chloride (salt). In the case of fat-soluble vitamins such as vitamin A, and certain minerals such as iron which the body cannot so easily dispose of, excess stores can ultimately be life-threatening. Athletes, therefore, need to take special care with regard to the dangers of over-indulgence, especially when it comes to diet supplements. Regular monitoring of body-weight can provide information about meeting nutrient requirements or meeting them to excess!

Indeed there is the *Recommended Amounts of Food Energy and Nutrients for Groups of People in the UK* (DHSS, 1979) which provides a useful guide. There is no evidence that sportspeople need any more than non-sportspeople, providing that they are eating a good variety of foods which will meet their energy needs. These needs may well vary from season to season and during different training periods. The total amount of food which is consumed may therefore also vary.

In summary, the overall needs of the athlete in training will be both variable and, to that athlete, unique. This variation may be masked by the ability of the individual to adapt to different levels of nutrition, but it is essential that such adaptation is not allowed to mask impending deficiency. Sportspeople and their coaches must remain vigilant.

WHAT'S IN FOOD?

Food is a mixture of nutrients: fat, carbohydrate, protein, vitamins and minerals. Everyone needs these nutrients in the same way. Eating food ultimately enables these nutrients to be made available for our bodies. All naturally occurring foods contain nutrients, but in differing amounts (dependent upon the function which the food performed in the plant or animal). For example, leaves are not storage organs and so their energy content is low. Meat, however, is muscle and so has a high protein content.

In Fig 64 there is a list of foods and some of the nutrients they contain. A more comprehensive list is given in the *Manual of Nutrition* (HMSO, 1985). This list is not exhaustive; if you want to learn more, you should consult a food composition table (*see* Further Reading). You should also remember that many foods may contain significant amounts from more than one group, for example a piece of apple pie contributes to the carbohydrate, fat, protein, vitamin and mineral content of the diet.

Sources of Carbohydrate

(Milk and milk products also provide significant amounts of calcium).

1 glass of milk   Supplies about 8g protein, 12g CHO, 8g fat, 150kcals.

For reduced energy and fat:
1 glass skimmed milk or 1 carton plain yoghurt   Supplies about 8g protein, 12g CHO, 80kcals.

Cereals and legumes – high carbohydrate and some protein.
1 thin/medium slice white bread*
½ roll, bun, crumpet, teacake etc.
1 tbs white flour*
1 digestive biscuit
   (also contains one portion of fat)   Each portion supplies about
4 tbs unsweetened breakfast cereal*   2g protein, 15g CHO as starch
3 tbs baked beans* or other cooked   and 70kcals.
   bean*/pea*/lentil*
   (also contains one third of portion of
   'meat' protein)
3–4 tbs fresh/processed peas
1 tbs apple crumble/pie
   (also contains one portion of fat and
   one 'fruit' carbohydrate portion)

Fruit and vegetables – also supply important vitamins.
Small apple, pear, orange
½ small banana
10–12 cherries or grapes
2 medium plums, prunes, apricots,   Each portion supplies about
   dates (dried)   0–2g protein, 5–10g CHO as
1 tbs raisins, currants   sugars and 25–40kcals.
2 tbs any vegetable (except avocado –
   add four portions of fat)
1 small/medium potato, boiled or baked
   (if fried add one portion of fat)

Sources of Fat
Small scrap butter or margarine (5g)
1 tsp oil
2 tsp mayonnaise
1 slice fried streaky bacon
5 olives
10 roasted peanuts
2 tsp double cream

Each portion supplies about 5g fat, 45kcals.

Sources of Protein
Meat and fish – also rich sources of minerals.
60–85g cooked (not fried) meat* or oily fish
60g hard cheese
85g edam, gouda, brie or similar
3 grilled sausages (add one portion of fat)

Each portion supplies about 20–25g protein, 15–20g fat, 200–250kcals.

For reduced energy and fat:
60–85g cooked chicken (no skin), veal or rabbit
60–85g cooked liver*
60–85g white fish
60–85g tuna in brine or 4 pilchards
170g cottage cheese

Each portion supplies about 20–25g protein, 5g fat, 150kcals, but do not fry or add fat.

Sources of Thiamin or Vitamin B1
Milk and milk products	all milk and soya milk
Cereals and legumes	all legumes**, fortified (non-wholemeal) bread**, flour products and fortified breakfast cereals
Meat and fish	ham and pork products, liver
Fruit and vegetables	none
Other	brewers' yeast

Sources of Riboflavin or Vitamin B2
Milk and milk products	all types of milk**
Cereals and legumes	only fortified breakfast cereals
Meat and fish	liver
Fruit and vegetables	dark-green leafed vegetables
Other	brewers' yeast

Sources of Pyridoxine or Vitamin B6
Milk and milk products	none
Cereals and legumes	all legumes**

Meat and fish	beef, pork, lamb, tuna and salmon
Fruit and vegetables	bananas and potatoes
Other	nuts

Sources of Calcium

Milk and milk products	all milk**, cheese**, yoghurt
Cereals and legumes	fortified flour and products (not wholemeal), tofu
Meat and fish	salmon and sardines if bones consumed
Fruit and vegetables	dark-green leafed vegetables
Other	molasses and unhulled sesame seeds (as in tahini)

Sources of Iron

Milk and milk products	none
Cereals and legumes	fortified flour and products**, fortified breakfast cereals, all legumes**
Meat and fish	red meats**, liver**
Fruit and vegetables	dark-green leafed vegetables
Other	molasses, chocolate and cocoa

Sources of Zinc

Milk and milk products	cheese
Cereals and legumes	all legumes, bread, wholemeal flour and products
Meat and fish	meat**, liver, crab and shellfish
Fruit and vegetables	very small amounts in most fruit and vegetables
Other	nuts

* also rich in iron
**particularly rich source

Fig 64 Nutrients contained in typical portions of food.

THE NEED FOR FLUID, ENERGY AND NUTRIENTS

Fluid

Our bodies are about seventy per cent water, so in a 70kg person 49kg is water. Cells (the constituents of every living thing) and blood need water in order to dissolve and to carry nutrients. Even a slight reduction in body water of two to five per cent (1.5–3.5l, 3–6 pts) can cause a reduced efficiency in cellular function. Dehydration also does not allow the body sufficient water to cool itself and so the body may overheat. This makes us feel disorientated and undoubtedly reduces performance. Fluid balance or hydration must therefore be of prime importance to all sportspeople. Water is normally lost in three ways:

(i)   Through urine. This volume is increased by taking more water or by certain nutrients such as alcohol (which has a diuretic effect).
(ii)   Through the skin. This normally accounts for a small percentage, but during exercise can rise to over 3l per hour, depending on the intensity of exercise and the environmental conditions.
(iii) Through the lungs.

Water can also be lost abnormally in two ways:

(i)   Through diarrhoea. This may be caused by infection or by eating too much fibre or simple carbohydrate, which cannot be absorbed; they also cause water to be drawn into the gut from the body tissues (causing cell dehydration).
(ii)   Through fevers. Extra water is lost through the skin in order to reduce body temperature.

Clearly, it is important to avoid extra fluid loss and this means being cautious over consuming foods from dubious origins (including ice cubes) and choosing carbohydrate foods wisely. (See later in this chapter.)

Replacing the fluid lost during training and competition is vital. Our normal thirst mechanisms do not operate successfully at this level of loss and so are unreliable. Water loss therefore needs to be monitored actively, which means weighing before and after any exercise. The change in weight will reflect the loss of body water content – and this must be replaced. The best way to do this is to use a drink which is 'isotonic' to body fluids (the same concentration) or 'hypotonic' (weaker concentration): the drink should never be 'hypertonic' (more concentrated) because body fluid will be drawn into the gut to dilute it (see above). This causes (osmotic) diarrhoea and is counter-productive. It has been found that a solution of 2.5g of sugar per 100 ml (about ½oz per pint), 23 mg (1.0 mmol) of sodium per 100 ml (a very small pinch per pint), 20 mg (0.5 mmol) of potassium per 100 ml (a smaller pinch per pint), served cold (as from the fridge) in about half pint quantities is ideal. Fortunately a dilute solution of orange squash (two to three tablespoons per pint) is just about the correct concentration. If using a commercially prepared drink, it is wise to check the concentration, which should not be greater than those given above. Plain water is also acceptable. Whatever is chosen, it is important to consume a replacement amount. One litre weighs about 1kg (2lb) and is equivalent to about two pints. It takes some practice and training to consume the quantities required. A drink containing alcohol causes extra urinary loss of water (it is a diuretic) and so should be avoided. Pints of beer will not do and caffeine also has diuretic properties.

Finally, before competition, individuals should prepare for the fluid which is to be lost. By carefully monitoring losses during training and competitions it is possible to make some predictions and to consume some fluid to cover anticipated losses.

Requirements for Energy and Nutrients

The nutritional requirements of each athlete will depend on several factors, including age, sex and body-weight (growing children or teenagers need proportionally greater amounts of food than adults, while women need more iron than men and men need more energy because they often weigh more) and duration and intensity of exercise.

The above list is particularly applicable when considering the amount of energy required. It is less applicable with regard to the need for protein, minerals and vitamins.

ENERGY

Energy is derived from fat and carbohydrate (CHO) in food and, to a lesser extent, protein. The amount of energy in food is measured in units corresponding to the amount of heat that food would produce when it is 'burned' in the body. The heat produced can be thought of as providing the power to make the body work in much the same way as a coal fire produces heat to make steam to turn an engine. These units of 'heat' are calories. A calorie is a very tiny amount of heat and the amount in food is thousands of calories or kilocalories (kcals). Another unit which is used to measure the amount of energy in food is the joule – again a very tiny unit of 'work-energy' and so expressed in kilojoules (kJ). One kilocalorie is equivalent to 4.2 kilojoules (1kcal = 4.2kJ). Large amounts of kilojoules are expressed as megajoules (MJ) – there are 1,000kJ to a megajoule.

Energy in the food is used to do 'internal work'; it keeps the heart beating and the lungs and other organs working, even when we are asleep. This basic, essential requirement for energy is known as the Basal Metabolic Rate (BMR) and varies with body size. BMR has the first priority for energy, however much is ingested. The other basic needs for energy are the renewal of body tissues and the excretion of waste products. After these energy requirements have been met, dietary energy is used for 'external' work. The amount of external work performed can be moderated to fit the dietary energy supply. The energy devoted to the synthesis of new tissue can also be moderated as the extra energy required for the synthesis of 1kg (2lb) of new tissue has been estimated to be as high as 5000 to 7000 kcals (about 21 to 29.4 MJ) above normal dietary intake.

SOURCES OF ENERGY

Carbohydrates as Dietary Sources of Energy

Plants store their energy as carbohydrate (CHO). This is a term used to cover a variety of molecules which all have similar chemical properties. Some molecules are small, taste sweet and are known as simple, or sugary, carbohydrate. They include glucose, sucrose (sugar), fructose, maltose and lactose (although lactose is an anomaly since animals produce it in milk for their young). Some molecules are large, do not taste sweet and are called complex, or starchy, carbohydrate (the starches in bread, potatoes, rice and pasta are all complex). Finally, there are some forms of carbohydrate which we cannot digest or absorb, known as unavailable carbohydrate or dietary fibre. Eventually all dietary sources of the sugary and starchy carbohydrate, or available CHO, will be transformed into glucose in the blood.

Each gram of available CHO provides 4kcals of energy to the body. It is found in all foods of plant origin: cereals, fruit, vegetables (including pulses such as dried peas, beans and lentils) and to a limited extent in nuts (see Fig 64). Fruit and vegetables contain a very high percentage of water and the carbohydrate which is present is much diluted. For this reason these foods are less 'energy-dense', which also applies to other nutrients similarly 'diluted'. It also means that to consume a large amount of energy a great quantity of these foods needs to be eaten. This is useful for slimmers, but not necessarily for the person who requires a high energy intake in a hurry. However, foods made from cereal grains (bread, pasta and biscuits or cakes and so on) do not contain as much water and so are more energy-dense. Bread, breakfast cereals, pasta and rice are all rich sources of CHO and are relatively energy-dense.

Once the CHO is consumed it appears in the blood as glucose. This can then be used directly for energy or stored in the muscle or in the liver as glycogen, the 'animal equivalent' of starch – a very important source of energy to all animal cells. There is a finite amount of glycogen which can be stored, about 200g (7oz). The glycogen stored in the muscle probably determines the amount of work which can be done by that muscle, while any excess glucose is then made into fat and stored in the adipose tissue.

Fats as Dietary Sources of Energy

Fat is found in almost all foods, since it is an important part of the cell wall of all plant and animal tissue. Plants do not store energy as fat (except in nuts) so the amount of fat in plant sources of food will be very low. Animals, including humans, store energy in their bodies as fat; indeed an average woman may have 10 kg (22lbs) of fat in her body. This fat is stored in many places; in adipose tissue around vital organs, under the skin and amongst muscle fibres. Therefore meat or animal products such as eggs, milk and milk products all contain fat, often in significant amounts (see Fig 64).

Fat is energy-dense and supplies 9kcals per gram, more than twice as much per unit weight as CHO. Animal products do not contain as much water as fruit and vegetables and so are doubly more energy and nutrient-dense. Fat can also taste nice; think of the taste of fried mushrooms compared to boiled or the taste of buttered rather than dry toast! Eating fat is easy and because it is energy-dense it provides energy in small amounts of food; hence over-indulgence is easy, too. Active and busy athletes need this form of energy which can be eaten in a hurry, but the slimmer needs to beware!

Sources of Energy in the Diet and Long Term Health

The amount and type of food-energy we consume may influence our health. It is generally agreed that there is a weight–height ratio at which adults are fitter and less prone to develop various life-threatening diseases. The more fat you carry, the higher will be the ratio and the more likely are such diseases. A simple way to calculate whether your weight–height ratio is satisfactory is to use this internationally-accepted method: weight (kg) divided by height (metres) squared. This is termed the Body Mass Index (or BMI). The range thought to be acceptable is 17–25. If it is below the bottom end this is just as disturbing as if it too high. Lean people *may* be more agile and active around the court but if weight is reduced too far this indicates poor body reserves of nutrients because of a restrictive dietary intake. A very restrictive intake can lead to nutrient deficiencies which will ultimately affect performance.

This weight–height ratio (BMI) is a simple and quick test. However, it does not tell us how much of an individual is fat, and how much is lean (muscle) tissue. To find out the ratio of fat to lean tissue a more specific measurement has to be made. One method which can be used is based on

Fig 65 Estimating body fat with skinfold callipers

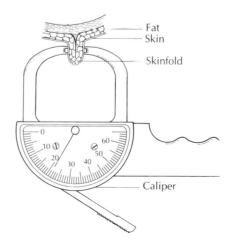

Fat
Skin

Skinfold

Caliper

the assumption that the fat under the skin is a fair reflection of total body fat. Using special skinfold callipers (see Fig 65) the amount of fat under the skin can be assessed. The total body fat can then be estimated by using a formula (Eisenman and Johnson, 1982). Women, for physiological reasons, have a higher percentage of body fat than men. The amount of fat which different people have varies and can be manipulated by use of exercise and diet, although the difference between men and women always remains. A list of measured body fats is given below:

Average adult man (20–50 years)	15–25 per cent fat
Average adult female (20–50 years)	26–35 per cent fat
Adult male tennis player	about 16 per cent fat
Adult female tennis player	about 20 per cent fat
Adult male (distance) runner	6–13 per cent fat
Adult female (distance) runner	15–19 per cent fat
Adult male volleyball player	about 19 per cent fat
Adult female volleyball player	about 23 per cent fat

The type of 'energy' consumed may have an effect on long term health. It is thought advisable to consume the majority of energy in the form of carbo-hydrate. Sugary carbohydrates can cause dental disease and therefore reliance should be on the complex, or starchy, carbohydrates. Fats are thought to be associated with heart disease and certain forms of cancer and for these reasons are best avoided in large amounts. The saturated fats found in animal sources are thought to be more harmful than the fats from vegetable sources which are largely unsaturated.

The development of certain diseases which mainly afflict people in the developed countries is probably due to a number of factors, but two of which are diet and lack of exercise. At this time it is difficult to say how 'protective' exercise, practised intensively, will be in the long term. Certainly, it is important for amateur and professional sportspeople to meet energy and food needs, which may mean eating more fat than would normally be advised for the general public. But what the effects on long-term health will be is uncertain at the present time.

PROTEIN

The requirement for dietary protein depends on several factors, including: the amount of muscle tissue present (the more muscle tissue, the more body protein there is to maintain and replace); the amount of new tissue synthesis (in the growth phase proportionally more protein is required and also there is increased demand for energy for synthesis); the amount lost through sweat and hair/skin loss.

Much controversy surrounds the nature and extent of the body's needs for protein. The body can become very efficient at conserving its store of protein which is found in every cell in the body. It would seem that sportspeople need the same amount of protein per kilogram of body-weight as untrained individuals, although they will need more if energy supplies are not sufficient to meet demand, since protein may be used to produce energy, if necessary. If there is insufficient energy in the diet then either food protein or body protein can be broken down and used in the same way as glucose. This, however, is very wasteful because once it is used for energy, it can not be used for body protein 'repair'.

The amount of protein required is closely related to how well energy supply meets demand; if enough carbohydrate and fat are consumed, protein requirements for sportspeople are no greater than for anyone else. Supplementary proteins are often used by sporting people but unlike the protein in food, they are not normally associated with energy – which means that they will not be well used. Work currently in progress at Leeds Polytechnic tends to indicate that the consumption of protein supplements can actually cause some athletes to reduce their overall food intake. This is clearly counter-productive in terms of maintaining an adequate energy and nutrient supply. Finally, it should be stated that protein will only be incorporated into muscle tissue if there is an appropriate training programme.

Amino acids are the tiny molecules which are joined together in particular sequences to make proteins. Proteins in hair will have a different sequence to the proteins in muscle (which is why hair doesn't look the same as muscle!). Once again all proteins contain all amino acids but in different amounts, depending on source and function. Generally, proteins from animal sources are nearer in amino acid pattern and proportion to our own bodies and needs. However, it is possible to get all these amino acids from plant sources. Vegetarians do this and are perfectly healthy. It is quite possible to rely on the cheaper vegetable sources of protein and, by mixing foods together, a better mix of amino acids is ensured. Putting cereals (bread, pasta, rice) together with nuts or pulses (dried beans, peas or lentils) creates a perfect complement of amino acids precisely the same as that found in the best sirloin!

How Much Protein?

The actual amount one needs is difficult to say. It is possible to give values for grams of protein but this is meaningless unless it is put into the context of food. Values for adults of 1–2g protein per kg of body-weight per day have been given. For someone who weighs 80kg the need for protein could be estimated at 80–160g per day. The values quoted in the DHSS recommended intake tables are comparable to this. About 40 kcals of energy are required per gram of protein. In the above example this would mean a food energy intake of between 3,200 and 6,400 kcals per day.

Food, however, is a mixture of nutrients and if the food in the diet provides, say, 3,000 kcals, then this amount is likely to contain at least 80g of protein and probably a lot more. It is very difficult to consume too little protein when eating a variety of foods (see Fig 64).

MINERALS AND VITAMINS

There is also little evidence to suggest that athletes have a greater bodily demand for vitamins compared to non-athletes. As has been said, food is a mixture of nutrients and as food intake rises (as it must do to support activity) then so does the level of vitamin supply through the food. A very bizarre diet indeed would have to be chosen for any deficiency to occur. However, it is possible to over-indulge in vitamin supplements — and this can be dangerous. It is becoming apparent that not only can over-indulging in vitamins (even vitamin C) lead to the development of harmful conditions, but also that such supplements affect the absorption of other nutrients. Individuals should take care and if supplements are thought necessary they should seek medical advice to confirm a positive need.

Minerals may be thought of in two groups, those which we require in relatively large amounts and those which we require in trace amounts. The former which are of importance here are sodium, potassium and calcium. Of those required in very small amounts the most important is iron. Sodium and potassium loss in sweat barely reaches levels whereby supplements are required above normal dietary intake and therefore they should not be considered outside the context of a normal varied diet.

There is, however, perhaps slightly more concern over adequate iron intake in athletes, due to the occasional occurrence of the condition known as 'sports anaemia', although it has not been described in volleyball players. The reason for this anaemia is not fully understood and may be a result of physical stress on the red blood cells or from abnormal losses of blood — both due to the intensity and prolonged effort of training and exercise. If anaemia is diagnosed then iron supplements will be advised. It would also be wise to make sure the diet contains iron-rich foods (see Fig 64).

A more serious cause of concern is the sportswoman (and it usually is the female) who deliberately restricts food intake to slim. When food is restricted, the supply of nutrients is reduced and this is especially critical with respect to iron and calcium, both of which are crucial to health in both the long and short term. Women who exercise hard and who limit their diet compensate for inadequate dietary supplies of iron by ceasing to menstruate. This is an indication that hormonal changes have occurred which are not normal. The other system which these changes affect is the synthesis and resynthesis of bone. On a low calcium intake (poor dietary supply) where some hormonal levels are low, bone is not effectively calcified and a condition known as 'osteoporosis' occurs. Weight-bearing exercises help to counteract this process to an extent, but the disturbing feature is that it is not known how the damage will manifest itself once serious sport is stopped. Women, in particular, should pay attention to their overall food intake, and especially to amounts of calcium and iron. Again, if the food-energy in a varied diet is in excess of 2,000kcals there should be no problem in meeting the requirements for iron and calcium. Fig 64 shows sources of calcium and other vitamins.

Overall, the athlete who is not restricting intake should not need any supplements of vitamins or minerals. In any event supplements should only be commenced when a deficiency is confirmed.

TRAINING SCHEDULES AND FOOD FOR COMPETITIONS

Rest periods are a vital part of successful training and allow the athlete to replenish energy and nutrient stores. Any schedule must, of course, allow time for the preparation and consumption of food. Obviously, without food we simply do not have the energy available to perform, and it must therefore be an essential part of the training schedule. Indeed it may well be that relaxation periods should become eating periods. 'Tapering' of exercise before competition allows for just this repletion phase. Productivity of training might well be improved if coaches and athletes were to give more thought to rest and food periods.

Timing of meals should be such that the major part of digestion is complete before activity commences. Fat and protein foods on the whole take longer to move through the stomach and small intestine (about 2–4 hours). Carbohydrate and cold foods are much quicker (about 1–2 hours, depending on the size of the meal). Sportsmen and women need to eat after a training session and good anticipation of food needs is essential. As it may not always be possible to consume a full meal, it may be sensible to take your own food (i.e. some sandwiches and a flask of fluid to provide the essential nutrient and fluid replacement). If you do have to eat out then carbohydrate in the form of baked potatoes, pizza or pasta makes the most sensible food – meals and snacks should always be based on the starchy carbohydrates, since they are more effective at repleting glycogen stores lost through exercise.

TRAINING FOR VOLLEYBALL

Training for volleyball, primarily a sport performed under aerobic conditions, mainly aims to enhance the cardiovascular system and muscle. This ensures efficient and continuous supply of 'fuel' and oxygen to the working muscles over a long period. Training sessions at sub-maximal work-load – aerobic training – also condition the body to use its fat stores as the major fuel. This is important, especially under match conditions, as the store of fat in the body is much greater than CHO and will therefore last for longer. However, fat is not the sole fuel and some CHO must also be used; this usage becomes proportionally greater as the intensity of the exercise increases – usually towards the end of a match or training session. It is the reserve of stored CHO present at this time that will determine the duration of intense work. For training sessions that are longer than an hour the amount of stored CHO (glycogen) determines the intensity of the work that the muscles can do. Power becomes increasingly difficult to generate in muscles that have diminishing amounts of available glycogen.

Volleyball players need stamina not only to see them through a long event but also for 'explosive' bursts of energy. These burses demand anaerobic metabolism, when the only fuel source is glucose (glycogen). Training sessions therefore aim both to build muscles and to train them to work and tolerate anaerobic conditions. Each exercise will normally be carried out to exhaustion. This conditions the muscles to anaerobic metabolism and by its nature depletes glycogen.

Training also seems to effect a change in the efficiency with which muscles store glycogen; it has been observed that training brings about swift, efficient repletion of stores, but only if muscles have a plentiful dietary supply. Generally, however, starchy carbohydrate may well be better at replacing the lost glycogen.

Aerobic conditioning requires long training sessions which are also expensive in terms of energy usage; it is therefore essential to take time to eat properly during this training. Concentrated sources of CHO are important (see Fig 64) as well as high energy foods (i.e. containing fat) such as chocolate, rich cakes, nuts and biscuits. Drinks or soups are also useful, especially those using milk and adding sugar, eggs or cream. Nor should you forget to replace the fluids which will have been used up in vigorous training.

Athletes in volleyball may also need to consider their lean–fat ratio – carrying too much fat can impede mobility. This consideration of excess body fat is an important part of training, but it is vital that the level of body fat achieved be easily maintained; constant dieting does not afford the energy for effective training.

Competition

As competition time approaches, the will to win must be combined with the suggested training programme. Diet can have a role in this, but food eaten before competition has little effect on immediate performance; it can in fact be detrimental. It is rather the extended period of preparation, training and diet which will affect performance on the day. Unlike food, it is imperative to drink before a competition since lack of fluids – or dehydration – may prevent you even finishing the match.

How to Arrive Ready to Compete

The message of this chapter has been to ensure that you get the 'energy books balanced', which means ensuring that energy is replaced in the working muscle. If this becomes part of the training schedule then relaxing before the event and allowing the body muscles to recoup their energy reserves takes place quite naturally; that is to say you should 'taper' the training schedule.

In fact, it can be quite unproductive to follow an unusually high carbohydrate diet for several days before the event, as this can lead to discomfort and diarrhoea. By careful measurement of an athlete's food intake it has been shown how very difficult it is for the individual actually to judge by how much he or she is increasing his or her intake. More often than not CHO intake is raised but the contribution to energy intake from fat is lowered, and so the individual is unable to achieve a sufficiently high overall energy intake. This means that instead of the carbohydrate being stored, it may be used for the essential work of body maintenance (so that glycogen storage is less than expected). The message here is that good dietary habits should develop and support training. This will also be highly suitable for immediate preparation for competition (which is often of shorter duration than the training sessions).

The planning of meals and snacks before or during a competition also needs consideration. As already mentioned it is vital to have the intestine as free as possible from the process of digestion; meals should therefore be finished at least two (preferably four) hours before competing, for the anticipation of competition may reduce intestinal function. Individuals should carefully plan those meals which they feel will be most beneficial. The content of the meals is largely irrelevant in terms of providing energy, which should have been taken care of 12–48 hours beforehand, although sugary snacks should be avoided as these may delay the release of internal energy (see below). It would also be wise to avoid those foods which are known to produce flatulence as this can be very uncomfortable during an event.

There are two factors which affect the utilisation of fuel. Firstly, taking something sugary about 45 minutes before starting an event will 'catch the body out', as it will be expecting to store food or nutrients and not to mobilise fuel. Moreover, the hormones which act to control body chemistry will not promote energy release, which can be very unfortunate for the athlete about to start a match! Secondly, the type of training will have determined how the individual responds to the demands of the exercise (i.e. whether or not fat is predominantly 'burned', so sparing glycogen).

Some ergogenic (or exercise-enhancing) aids may be tried. One which has some use, provided it is not misused by overindulgence, is caffeine. Consumed about 45 minutes before exercise, it has two effects: firstly, it is a stimulant and reduces the feeling of effort and secondly, it causes fatty acids to be 'mobilised' and used as fuel, so sparing glycogen.

The amount of caffeine which has been found to produce this effect is 4mg per kg of body weight. Caffeine is found in chocolate to a small extent and in drinks in the following amounts:

1 cup (200ml) cola		35mg
1 cup (150ml) coffee	instant	70mg
	percolated	120mg
	filter	160mg
1 cup (150ml) tea		50mg

Caffeine is a drug. If it is given in large and uncontrolled amounts it can produce vascular changes which may be harmful. In addition, at everyday doses it can have a pronounced diuretic effect which is not particularly desirable when hydration is required.

Hydration is probably the single most important factor for success on the day. It is essential that fluid is replaced little and often throughout the match. The concept of fluid with a suitable concentration to ensure maximum absorption has been discussed earlier. Remember it may be counter-productive to include glucose in the solution, the energy should already be stored in the muscles.

Eating between matches should follow the basic rules outlined earlier and be completed at least two hours before the next competition, although some digestion and absorption of food does occur at submaximal levels of exercise. Each individual should note what types of food can be easily digested between matches and those which bring about indigestion.

Summary

Eating for volleyball should become part of the training schedule. Limiting food is often counter-productive and monitoring of food and fluid intake as well as body-weight should be routine.

4 Injury Prevention

CLASSIFICATION OF INJURY

In order to prevent injuries it is preferable to understand why they occur and where they occur in the body. An injury may be due to an external force (extrinsic injury) or to a force within the body (intrinsic injury). Extrinsic injuries happen when a player collides with an object such as a wall, the floor, a piece of equipment, or even another player. They can also be caused by an object hitting the body such as a volleyball. Intrinsic injuries may happen without any particular cause (incidental injury) but they are more likely to occur when the training load is rapidly increased in intensity and frequency (overuse injury). Most injuries tend to occur quite suddenly (acute injury), but fortunately tend to settle very quickly. However, an acute injury may become a chronic injury, which is usually more difficult to treat and takes longer to overcome. You are far more likely to get injured towards the end of a training session or match, when you become tired, than at any other time, so take more care as you become fatigued.

SITE OF INJURY

Sports injuries may occur anywhere in the body, such as in muscles, tendons (pullies attached to the bone from the muscles), tenosynovia (the protective sheaths around a tendon), ligaments (fibrous bands joining two bones together at a joint), joints and bones.

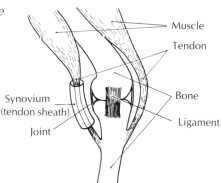

Fig 66 Physiological representation of the knee.

Muscle

Tendon

Synovium
(tendon sheath)

Joint

Bone

Ligament

It is helpful to grade the injuries into three groups:

(i)   Group A. Minimal damage when bruising only occurs and there is no major disruption to the muscle, tendon or ligament etc. Small blood vessels are damaged, however, and leak blood which forms a bruise (haematoma).
(ii)   Group B. Some disruption of the tissues takes place and a sprain, strain, partial tear or partial rupture takes place in a muscle, tendon (tendonitis), tendon sheath (tenosynovitis), ligament or bone (stress fracture). Stress fractures of bones can be likened to the cracks in a piece of wire which has been repeatedly bent – at first the wire looks strong but eventually, if stressed enough, it can break right through.
(iii) Group C. Complete ruptures of muscles, tendons, and ligaments, fractured or broken bones and dislocated joints.

Further classification of injury can be as shown in the following table:

Extrinsic (outside force)
  collisions
  falls
  equipment

Intrinsic (internal force)
  incidental (no cause)
  overuse
  acute
  chronic

AVOIDANCE OF INJURIES

The basic rule for avoiding injury is to improve your own fitness through increased speed, strength, endurance and flexibility, as outlined in Chapter 2. Using the training programme in a sensible progressive way reduces the chances of sustaining intrinsic and overuse injuries. Skill is not only important in making a better all-round player but also enables the player to avoid injury through inappropriate technique. For example, practise your roll in back-court recovery or try sliding in a dive at the same time as keeping the chin up – so allowing your body to absorb energy over a greater area of its surface. Cupping the hands correctly when passing reduces the chance of your fingers being stubbed or bent back. When digging, in order to cut down on injuries to the hands, wrists and forearms, the arms should be straight but not rigid, the ball rebounding off an area just above the wrists with the thumbs pointing down.

Warm-Up and Cool-Down

Warm-up is essential not only in preparation for matches but also in training. By gradually increasing the intensity of work and building up the number of skills to be rehearsed the body and mind are both being warmed up. The muscles are controlled by electrical impulses fed to them from the brain and this system needs tuning and adjusting – just as the muscles need warming up. Equally as important is the cool down or unwind when more emphasis is put on flexibility in order to test for any minor injury that may have occurred during exercise.

Gentle rhythmic movement also helps in flushing out the waste products of metabolism from the muscles that build up during high intensity exercise. Muscle stiffness the following day can be reduced by performing a regular post-match or post training drill of stretching and low intensity exercise (see Chapter 2).

Protection

Most extrinsic injuries can be avoided by taking sensible precautions – such as checking the safety of the training venue and any equipment that is used in it. The volleyball hall should be well ventilated, well lit and with any sharp edges, radiators or nearby walls padded with foam. Doors and windows should be secured and other recreational equipment stored correctly and well out of the way of the court. Floor surfaces can be made of several different types of material, but check for splinters or wear in the surface and ensure the floor area is free from water and sweat.

The supporting posts of the net should be of the approved type and be fitted into sockets in the floor or firmly attached to the floor by brackets. Ensure that there are no supporting wires, ropes or strings which are not permitted and that the net is set at the correct height.

The volleyball should be of the approved type – heavy balls may cause more injuries to the fingers, wrists and forearms. Children may need to start with lighter, smaller, plastic balls. The clothing you wear should be well fitting, not too tight so that it rubs causing abrasions nor too loose so that it gets in the way of free movement. Tops should be long sleeved to prevent friction burns when diving or rolling. Knee pads can give additional protection when receiving serves, digging or diving and some players may find elbow pads helpful.

Shoes should be matched to the type of surface to be played on so that neither excessive grip nor sliding occurs, and they should have good shock-absorbing qualities for landing from jumps. New shoes should be worn in slowly and not used for the first time in a match or for a long training session in case chafing and blistering results. Try to wear new shoes around the house for a few days before training in them.

Some players may wish to strap their fingers, ankles or feet – particularly if they have been injured in the past. The strapping needs to be inelastic (such as zinc oxide) in order to support the joints adequately and must be taken off after exercise to allow a full range of movement to take place. A trained physiotherapist can show you how to apply the tape.

Control

Many of the rules of the game and the regulations controlling the use of training venues have been devised to prevent injury. It is therefore prudent to observe these rules for your own safety. Always try to play with people of similar physique and ability. The tactics of the game need to be learned and discussed with the coach and other players, thus preventing unnecessary collisions. One of the commonest volleyball injuries is a sprained ankle which occurs when a blocker lands from a jump on the spiker's, or another blocker's, foot.

Self-control – in various guises – plays an important role in preventing and reducing injury. Try to organise your day in advance; adequate time should be allowed for meals with at least two hours elapsing before training after a large meal while most athletes need a minimum of eight hours' sleep each night – and time must be allocated for training, eating, studying or working. Fatigue will set in if not enough time is allowed for adequate rest between training sessions; indeed this is the cause of many sports injuries. Regular showering or bathing after training and frequent washing of kit will help reduce the incidence of fungal infections of the skin. Do not borrow other peoples' clothing or towels and make sure you always have clean dry clothing to change into after a training session. You should not smoke, not only for the obvious health reasons but also because the nicotine in cigarettes attaches itself onto the oxygen-carrying component of the red blood cells (haemoglobin) so reducing the availability of oxygen for the muscles. This effect lasts for up to three weeks after the last cigarette has been smoked.

Check-List for injury prevention.

(i)   Environment: clothes; shoes; equipment; surfaces.
(ii)   Control: training/match rules; physique; tactics.
(iii) Fitness: skill; strength; speed; endurance; flexibility.
(iv)   Self-discipline: warm-up; diet; sleep; smoking; hygiene.

MEDICAL PROBLEMS

Frequently it may be illness and not injury that prevents the sportsman or woman from training. Any volleyball player who has an infection, such as a heavy cold, a chest infection or flu, should not train or play, especially if the body temperature is elevated above normal (36.9°C, 98.4°F), or if the resting pulse rate is appreciably higher than normal. You will not be able to perform well and certainly will not get any beneficial training effect if you continue to train at this stage; you also run the risk of the infection getting worse and the heart muscle being affected (myocarditis). Rest is essential until the illness passes. Low-grade chronic infections of the teeth, skin or sinuses, for example, may prevent you performing at peak level and treatment should be sought earlier rather than later. Some virus infections such as glandular fever may linger on for weeks and regrettably there is no treatment – so you must remain patient until the illness passes, returning gradually to full training.

Dehydration

A reduction in body weight of one per cent through sweat results in a ten per cent reduction in work capacity; likewise a two per cent loss will result in a twenty per cent reduction in work capacity. It is therefore vital that any sweat lost is adequately and promptly replaced by water, not only to enhance performance, but also to prevent injury. Some people, particularly when training regularly in the summer in hot gyms, may become chronically dehydrated with a subsequent reduction in body weight, reduced urine output and a rise in resting pulse. Regular weighing and checking the volume and colour of the urine should ensure that dehydration does not become a problem (thirst alone is not a reliable indicator of dehydration).

OVERTRAINING

This condition is difficult to spot and may creep up on the athlete and coach without either being aware of what is happening. It usually occurs when the

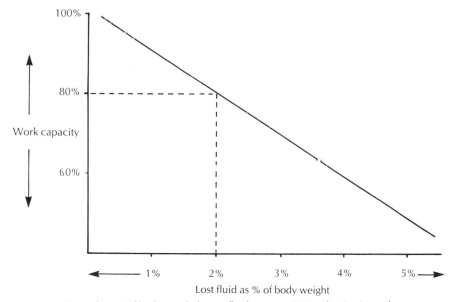

Example: 2% of body weight lost as fluid causes a 20% reduction in work capacity.

Fig 67 The relationship between loss of body fluid and reduction in work capacity.

sportsman or woman increases the training load both in frequency and intensity, not allowing time enough to eat, sleep, study or work. As the performance drops off the athlete tries to compensate by increasing the training load only to suffer further deterioration in performance, starting down the slippery slope and getting involved in a vicious circle of increased work and poor performance. The only cure is to rest for four days and increase both the fluid and carbohydrate intake, resisting the temptation to restart training after only one or two days when feeling a little recovered.

WOMEN

Women who have frequent heavy periods may lose enough iron to make themselves anaemic. When anaemia occurs the red blood cells are unable to carry sufficient oxygen to the muscles, resulting in tiredness both on and off the court. The doctor can easily correct this deficiency and advice should be sought as early as possible. Some women who undergo a lot of endurance training may cease to have periods, particularly if they reduce their body fat. This condition is known as amenorrhoea and is quite normal in these circumstances; periods will return when the training load is decreased. Pregnant women can safely continue to train and compete until they start feeling uncomfortable; indeed regular exercise in pregnancy results in healthier babies and easier childbirth for the mother.

CHILDREN

Bones continue to grow up to the age of eighteen in males and sixteen in females. However, during growth the bones are not strong enough for the muscles and tendons attached to them, so heavy weight-training and repetitive high-load training should not be performed by pre-pubertal children. In some children the points at which tendons are attached to bones become inflamed, swollen and tender. This may happen just below the knee (Osgood Schlatters condition) or at the back of the heel (Severs condition). The only treatment is to reduce the loading to that particular point by cutting down on the training until the condition settles.

Children can train on resilient surfaces such as grass and during training the use of shock-absorbing heel inserts made of sorbothane will prove effective in relieving pain. Children develop power and 'explosive force' after puberty and so power training should not be undertaken until after this time. Training with very light weights will, however, help with the technical skills of heavier weight-training later on.

VETERANS

Older sportspeople are not especially prone to particular injuries, but as age advances, the chances of their being injured increase and it takes them longer to recover from injury. If you go back to volleyball late in life, having had a few years away from sport, start gently with a gradual increase in the frequency and intensity of each session. Secondary injuries may occur in joints previously damaged in earlier years, for example injuries such as osteoarthritis of the knee joint may develop long after a torn cartilage has been removed. These secondary injuries may prevent you from doing as much training as you would like, but you will have to adjust to this and perhaps supplement your usual training with swimming and cycling.

TRAVEL

When travelling away from home, whether abroad or in your own country, you may experience difficulty in sleeping, especially during the first few nights. A muscle relaxant may prove helpful at this time and your doctor should be able to help if it becomes a problem. Stay clear of new and untried exotic foods, keep to your usual diet if at all possible and wash any fruit or salads in clean water before eating them. Check that the water supply is safe to drink and if not, consume bottled water only. When going to a hot climate the body takes ten days or so to acclimatise to the heat. After this period the salt content of the sweat is reduced and stabilised so all that is required is a little extra salt during the first few days, although you should not take salt tablets which can make you feel ill.

If you have a fair skin, you should keep out of the sun, and even if you tan easily you should still avoid sunbathing as you may become dehydrated. Ideally you should always wear long sleeves and long trousers at dusk and at dawn to avoid insect bites and should also use plenty of insect repellent. Check with your doctor to find out whether any special vaccinations are required well in advance of your trip. A travel check-list will include: vaccinations; food; water; heat acclimatisation; sleep disturbance; jet lag.

DOPING

It is your responsibility as an athlete to ensure that you do not abuse drug-testing regulations whether intentionally or by error. Mistakes can occur when over-the-counter pain killers, cough mixtures, anti-diarrhoea medicines and nasal decongestants are used which may contain small amounts of codeine and ephedrine. Both drugs are on the banned list and will show up in urine as a positive dope test. Check with the governing body or the Sports Council's Drugs Advisory Group for an up-to-date list of drugs you can and cannot take.

FIRST AID

If you are a coach you have a responsibility to know the basic procedures of resuscitation. When a serious casualty occurs your first aim is to save life before worrying about the extent of any sports injury:

(i)   Check the airway and remove any object in the way of air entering the lungs; remove any false teeth or mouth guards, clear the mouth of vomit or chewing gum and loosen any clothing around the throat. Extend the neck fully in order to prevent the tongue flopping down against the back of the throat.

(ii)   Check that breathing is now going on, if not start CPR (cardiopulmonary resuscitation) by giving the kiss of life. Breathe into the mouth of the casualty at the same time as pinching his or her nose to prevent air escaping from it.

(iii)   Check the circulation by feeling for a pulse; if you cannot detect it, start compressing the chest wall firmly four times for each of your breaths until the casualty starts breathing and regains his or her pulse, or until the ambulance arrives.

(iv)   After the patient has regained consciousness or started breathing by him or herself, check for any bleeding. If there is bleeding, apply firm pressure with a gauze swab or handkerchief for five minutes (in most cases this will be sufficient to stop blood loss from most major blood vessels). You can then start assessing the extent of any injury and try to relieve pain by placing the casualty in a stable position on their side, splinting any obvious fractures. Ideally you should always check beforehand where the nearest telephone is and send someone to summon the ambulance in order to evacuate the injured person.

Treatment of Sports Injuries

The aim of treatment is to reduce the amount of damage already done, relieve pain and promote healing. When a sports injury or soft-tissue injury occurs, small blood vessels become torn and blood escapes causing bruising and swelling. Action should be taken to help reduce the amount of blood escaping and so cut down on the size of the swelling, both of which hinder repair and rehabilitation. A mnemonic (RICE) is useful in this context.

Rest
Ice
Compression
Elevation

Rest is required for the first twenty-four hours following an injury in order to prevent further bleeding.

   Ice is applied to the injury for ten minutes every two hours in the first twenty-four hours. This reduces pain, swelling and further bleeding. The ice should be wrapped in a damp tea-towel and must not come into direct contact with the skin; if it does an ice burn may occur. If ice is not available, cold water, or a bag of frozen peas from the freezer will do!

Compression of the injury by a firmly applied crêpe bandage prevents further blood escaping and reduces the size of any swelling. The bandage should not be too tight and you may need to reapply the crêpe if it becomes too loose or too tight in the first twenty-four hours.

Elevation assists in the 'drainage' of swelling and the prevention of further loss of blood. The affected limb should be raised above the level of your heart for twenty-four hours.

Treatment of Blisters

The treatment for blisters depends upon whether or not the skin overlying it is intact. If it is, the blister should be left well alone, but if the skin has been broken the blister should be 'deroofed' with a clean pair of scissors. This prevents infection setting in and also assists in the blister bed healing more rapidly, if perhaps a little more uncomfortably in the short term. While training, the blister should be covered with a dry, non-absorbent dressing, held in place by a piece of tape or strapping. While on the subject of first aid, the contents of any first-aid box should include: crêpe bandages; gauze squares; zinc oxide tape; plasters; cotton wool; triangular bandage; scissors; antiseptic solution; analgesic (pain-killing tablets); collar; splints. You should also have access to a stretcher, blanket and Brooks airway.

REHABILITATION

Early rehabilitation of most injuries should be encouraged in order to shorten the time taken to reach a full recovery. In the first twenty-four hours when 'RICE' is applied, gentle passive movements are made to assist in the drainage of any swelling and to prevent blood clots forming in the deep veins. After a further twenty-four hours, more active stretching exercises are performed followed by strengthening exercises. The muscles around an injury rapidly lose power and the co-ordination of muscle movements also worsens within a few hours of the injury being sustained. As the muscles regain power, re-education of volleyball skills become a priority, eventually allowing a return to training and to playing matches.

Models for Rehabilitation

(i) **Group A injuries.** Bruising only has occurred and all that is generally required is the application of RICE in the first twenty-four hours followed by a fairly rapid resumption of normal training.
(ii) **Group B injuries.**
(a) Ligaments/joints. A sprained ligament on the outside of the ankle joint is

the most common volleyball injury. The principles used for the rehabilitation of this particular injury may also be applied to other injuries.

After twenty-four hours (when RICE is applied) try to walk on the injured side without a limp in order to stretch any scar tissue that is forming into its correct anatomical alignment. Initially this may mean that you will have to walk very slowly, before progressing first to normal walking pace and then to walking and jogging on grass five to ten metres at a time, slowly increasing the distance to twenty-five, fifty, seventy-five and then one hundred metres. When you have reached this stage, continue jogging for up to four hundred metres before starting a few sprints of five to ten metres followed by sprints of twenty-five, fifty, seventy-five and one hundred metres. Now run backwards and start weaving and jumping to strengthen the ankle further.

Nerves are often damaged in a ligament injury and so lose their ability to tell the brain where in space your foot is. These nerves need to be 're-educated' and the best way to do so is by doing balance exercises.

These positional or 'proprioceptive' exercises must be done at the same time as the stretching and strengthening drills. Start by trying to 'stork-stand' on your injured leg, then close your eyes; after this try throwing a ball up into the air and catching it again while still balancing on one leg. The degree of difficulty can be increased by standing on a balance or wobble board. When you can happily manage all of this regime for fifteen to twenty minutes, you are fit enough to resume normal training. If, having done this, your ankle still does not feel stable, or if you are unable to play, then advice from a sports clinic or qualified physiotherapist should be sought.

(b) Muscles and tendons. Torn thigh muscles (quadriceps) may occur in volleyball when jumping vigorously for the ball or landing awkwardly from a jump. The aim of rehabilitation is to prevent shortening of the muscle or tendon by inappropriate scar tissue formation (scar tissue may contract for several weeks after an injury).

Following the usual RICE application in the first twenty-four hours, you should gently stretch the quadriceps muscle for ten minutes each morning and evening and for a minute every hour during the day. As gentle stretching becomes less uncomfortable, more active stretching and static strengthening exercises should be undertaken, followed by dynamic exercises with increased loadings. Accordingly, start with straight-leg exercises, then with a bent knee, and then add weights of two to four pounds attached to the ankle while bending and straightening the knee. After this, the routine of jogging, sprinting, weaving, running backwards and jumping, together with balance exercises, (as used for the ankle injury) should again be followed.

(iii) **Group C injuries.** Bone fractures and dislocated joints. Most fractures or broken bones, together with joint dislocations, are major injuries and need a minimum of six weeks' immobilisation before any rehabilitation can commence (they also require close medical supervision). Stress fractures, however, need only to be rested for three weeks before gentle progressive training is resumed. If you think you have a stress fracture you should stop training and seek medical advice.

5 Mental Training

A comprehensive book on volleyball would not live up to its title if there was no chapter on mental training! Yet it is ironic that despite the widespread recognition of the importance of mental fitness in sport, very few practical training books on specific sports make more than a passing reference to such issues. Even so, there are now quite a few books on mental training in sport, some of which are listed at the end of this book. The complete player, therefore, will be someone who trains physically *and* mentally!

In his book entitled *The Pursuit of Sporting Excellence* (1986) David Hemery recalls his numerous interviews with a wide range of sport's highest achievers. In response to his question 'to what extent was the mind involved in playing your sport?' he reported; 'the unanimous verdict was couched in words like "immensely", "totally", "that's the whole game", "you play with your mind", "that's where the body movement comes from" '. In short, we all recognise the importance of having the right mental approach in sport just as we recognise the importance of physical factors. The purpose of this chapter, therefore, is to present a selection of some mental training skills relevant to volleyball players (although many of the skills are relevant to most people in a wide variety of sports). Before outlining some of these skills, it is important to dispel some of the myths surrounding mental training in sport.

MYTHS AND TRUTHS

Myth 1 'You only need a sports psychologist if you have mental problems.' If that was the case then, extending the argument, we would only need to train physically when we were trying to recover from injury! There is no difference between practising physical and mental skills – they should both be practised regularly as a positive aid to performance and not just to offset 'problems' (although they can usefully be employed for this as well).

Myth 2 'All good athletes have a natural mental toughness and don't need to practise mental skills.' Certainly some people will have better mental qualities than others (in exactly the same way that some people are more physically gifted than others) but that does not mean that mental training will not help. Even the Daley Thompsons of this world put in tremendous amounts of physical training despite being clearly physically gifted people. These days natural ability is not good enough.

Myth 3 'Mental skills cannot be trained or developed.' This is similar to the last myth, and it, too, is incorrect. All skills, whether physical or mental, can be improved with appropriate practice.

Mental training may not be fully accepted by all people in sport, but the preceding argument may have convinced you that it is illogical to expect physical training to be the only training in sport given that many games are won and lost on mental attitudes and abilities. Many years ago it was considered slightly odd – even 'unsporting' – to train more than about three days a week. That attitude has long since gone, but has been replaced with a reluctance to accept regular mental training as a part of contemporary sport. In a few years time, perhaps, we will look back at such an odd attitude with a sense of amusement.

COMPONENTS

In Chapter 2 the various components of physical fitness training were outlined and it was stated then that fitness was best defined in terms of its constituent parts. In the same way, it would be naive to say that mental training is made up of just one factor. It is a term given to a number of different components but it will not be possible to cover all of these in detail in such a short space and interested readers are referred to Further Reading at the back of this book. What will be done here, however, is to outline the basic features of five topics, which are:

(i)   Relaxation and the control of stress.
(ii)   Mental imagery.
(iii)   Concentration and mental control.
(iv)   Self-confidence.
(v)   Team-work.

The background to each of these areas will be explained in brief, including examples from volleyball, and then some practical mental training exercises in each area will be outlined. However, it should be noted that not all mental skills can be easily taught by coaches without training – although the exercises outlined here have been chosen for simplicity and safety. It is recommended, however, that if mental exercises are used, they are introduced by a registered sports psychologist of the British Association of Sports Sciences (*see* Useful Addresses). Coaches are also advised to attend courses on sports psychology run by the National Coaching Foundation (address also at the end of the book).

Relaxation and the Control of Stress

Relaxation is a much misunderstood concept in mental training, many players thinking that if relaxation skills are needed at all, they are only needed before a game. Clearly, being too relaxed is not a good idea, nor is being too tense. The answer, therefore, is to control the 'on–off switch' of the body. On most radios the on–off switch also controls the volume. Seeing that as humans we are 'on' all of the time, the essence of controlling the on–off switch is to control the volume. One way to do this is to learn relaxation skills, of which there are many. Other mental skills, such as mental imagery and concentration, are also dependent on being able to control the relaxation and activation (arousal) of the body.

Relaxation not only facilitates rest and recovery in sport, but also can have a more immediate effect on performance through reducing anxiety and muscle tension. Moreover, this can relate to self-confidence – another mental skill to be discussed later.

Arousal is the 'intensity-aspect' of our behaviour since we often refer to being under-aroused (e.g. drowsy, sleepy) or over-aroused (e.g. over-excited, panicky). In sport it is easy to get over-aroused with the excitement of the situation, for example the rugby player who is so 'psyched-up' at the kick-off that he charges down the field only to discover that he has over-run the ball by thirty metres! This shows that over-arousal is not necessarily a good thing in sport and can badly affect concentration.

There are many different types of relaxation skill that can be learned, including breathing exercises, muscle tense–relax exercises and meditation. After a time, you will develop your own preference and there is no one technique that can be recommended more than another. Two techniques will be outlined here, and others can be found in the books to which I have already referred. It should be recognised that not everyone is suited to starting these exercises especially those with abnormal blood pressure or a history of cardiorespiratory health problems, asthmatics, and those suffering acute anxiety states, who should all be referred to their doctor beforehand.

Deep Muscle Relaxation

This simple technique requires you to lie on the floor with your arms and legs stretched out. Gradually reduce your breathing rate to a slow yet comfortable rate, start saying the word 'relax' to yourself as you breathe out. Close your eyes when you feel ready to do so, but do not force it. After about ten exhalations, coupled with the word 'relax', focus your attention on your left leg. Imagine it getting gradually heavier and heavier as you become increasingly more relaxed. Imagine your leg sinking into the mat (concentrate on this for about a minute). Now shift your attention to your right leg and repeat the exercise. This can also be done for the left and right arms in succession. After this you should be quite relaxed and feeling 'heavy' – with little or no muscular tension. Slowly sit up, stretch and return to normal activities.

This should be practised for short spells initially as your concentration is likely to be poor. Five minutes may not sound very much but will be plenty for the first session. This form of deep relaxation is best performed several hours before competition to allow you plenty of time to increase the arousal level to the appropriate point for the game.

Progressive Muscle Relaxation

Progressive muscle relaxation (PMR) is a well-known technique for learning the difference between relaxation and tension. It was developed in the 1930s by Edmund Jacobsen and is widely used in sport, health and other contexts today. Essentially, the technique is built upon the premise that you will be unable to relax effectively until you can first recognise tension. Consequently, the exercises are a series of tense–relax exercises designed to increase your awareness of muscular tension and relaxation, as illustrated in Fig 68. Below there is a PMR script which you can either have read to you or which can be recorded in a quiet, relaxed voice.

Relaxation Procedures

These procedures should be practised twice a day for about ten minutes at a time (evenings are often a good time to practise). The order of the steps involved is very important; however, the particular words or thoughts that the athlete uses to accomplish each step are not. For example, it is important that you relax prior to concentrating on bowling. When you are concentrating on relaxing your arms, we don't care if you say to yourself, 'Now I am going to release all the muscular tension in my hands, fingers, and forearms,' or if you say, 'Now I am going to relax the muscles in my hands, fingers, and arms.'

Prior to beginning the exercise, find a quiet, comfortable place where you will not be disturbed and where you can either sit or lie down. If you wear contact lenses, you may want to remove them. If you have on restrictive clothing (like a tie), you may want to loosen it. Make yourself comfortable with your hands at your sides or in your lap and you are ready to begin.

1 Close your eyes and take three deep breaths, inhaling and exhaling deeply and slowly. As you exhale, relax your entire body as much as you

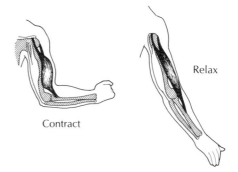

Fig 68 The tense–relax sequence of progressive muscle relaxation.

Contract

Relax

can. Continue to notice your breathing throughout the session. You will find that as you exhale, your relaxation will become deeper.

2   Now clench both your fists. Close them and squeeze them tighter and tighter together. As you squeeze them, notice the tension in your forearms, your hands, and your fingers. That's fine, now let them go, relax them. Let your fingers become loose and notice the pleasant feeling of heaviness in your arms and hands as the tension disappears. Feel the heaviness of your arms and hands as they rest against your body or the chair. That's fine, try it one more time, clench both fists and feel the tension, squeeze harder, hold the tension, now let go and completely relax.

3   Now bend your elbows, clench your fists, and flex your biceps. Flex them harder, hold the tension and study it. Now unbend your elbows, relax your hands, get your arms back in a comfortable position, study how your arms feel as you completely let go and relax them.

4   Now straighten your arms and flex the triceps muscle in the back of your upper arms. Hold the tension, increase it, squeeze harder, study the tension. That's fine, now relax, return your arms to a comfortable position and enjoy the release from the tension. Enjoy the feelings, and even when you feel completely relaxed, try and let go even more.

5   Now clench your teeth, feel the muscles tightening in your neck and jaws. Once again, study the tension, clench your teeth tighter, tighter. Now relax your jaws, let your mouth open slightly, and feel your muscles loosen, feel the relief from the tension.

6   Pay attention to your neck muscles. Press your head back as far as it will go and feel the tension, now roll it straight to the right. Again feel the increase in the tension in your muscles. Move your head to the left, pressing hard and feeling the tension in your muscles. Hold the same position and study the tension. Now let your head move into a comfortable position and relax the muscles in your neck and shoulders. Notice the pleasant change as you feel the tension leaving your muscles. Pay attention to how your neck and shoulders feel when the muscles are relaxed.

7   Now pay attention to your breathing and relax your entire body. Breathe deeply and slowly, and as you exhale, relax all the muscles in your arms. Just let yourself go and completely relax. Let your mouth open slightly and relax the muscles in your face, jaw, and forehead. Relax the muscles in your neck and shoulders . . . Relax the muscles in your feet, your calves, and your thighs . . . That's fine . . . Just completely relax and let yourself go. Continue to breathe deeply and slowly, and enjoy the pleasant feeling of being completely relaxed.

8 At this time those of you who wish may practise rehearsing the sights and feelings that you associate with a particular pleasant activity. This practice should not last for more than four to five minutes.

9 Now, since you have relaxed so completely, it is best to take your time in moving around. Get out of this relaxed state by using three steps. First, count one and take a deep breath and hold it. Second, count two and stretch your arms and legs, then exhale. Third, count three and open your eyes. You should be wide awake and feeling very relaxed and comfortable.

Procedure Summary
1 Close your eyes and breathe deeply and slowly.
2 Relax the muscles in your forearms.
3 Relax your biceps.
4 Relax your triceps.
5 Relax your face, jaw, and forehead.
6 Relax your neck and shoulders.
7 Breathe slowly and relax your entire body.
8 Rehearse an activity.
9 Take a deep breath, stretch, and open your eyes.

Reprinted with permission from Nideffer, R. M. *The Inner Athlete* (Thomas Y. Crowell, 1976).

It is also possible to purchase relaxation tapes (available from the National Coaching Foundation). Fig 69 shows some of the exercises for PMR.

Prayer arm-push

Toe-curl (back)

Toe–curl (under)

Ankle (back)

Ankle (under)

Knees press

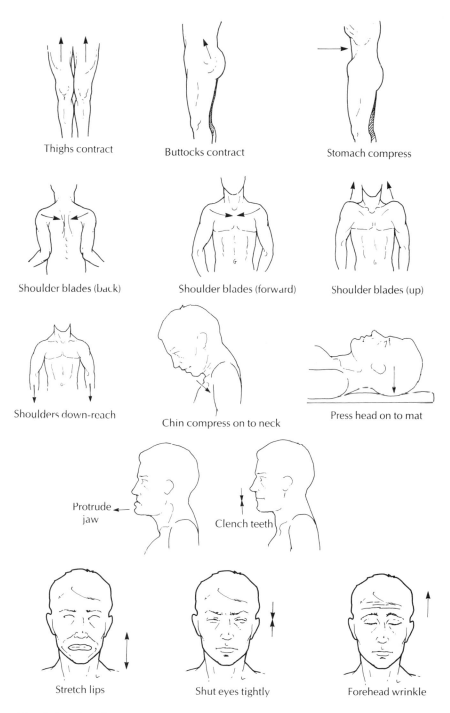

Fig 69 Exercises for tension recognition in PMR.

Fig 70 Optional enjoyment through matching challenge and skill (adapted from Csikszentmihalyi, M., Beyond Boredom and Anxiety, Jossey-Bass, 1975).

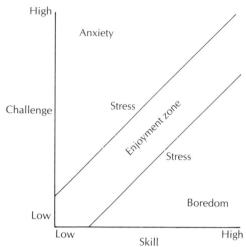

Relaxation, Anxiety and Stress

We have all experienced the unpleasantness of anxiety in sport; the nervousness before a big game, or the critical point in the match which could swing it either way. However, not all stress is bad. Stress actually refers to any situation when we are 'out of balance', such as when the task appears to be too difficult or too easy for us. (The latter will produce the stress of boredom, hence the diagram in Fig 70, which shows that optimum enjoyment is often the result of matching the challenge with the right level of skills; any imbalance could cause stress). The body prepares for stress through the 'fight–flight' reaction, which is the response of the body preparing for action with increased heart rate, breathing rate, adrenalin flow etc. This feeling could equally be fear or excitement, depending upon how you see the situation. If you hear footsteps rapidly approaching you from behind in a dark alley-way late at night you will react with fear if you think it is a mugger. However, if you think it is a jogger you will not react in the same way. In other words, your stress or anxiety response depends upon the way in which you see the situation. In volleyball, you will need to develop relaxation skills and a positive way of looking at the game when you become anxious.

Mental Imagery

The ability to visualise events and skills in volleyball is another important mental skill which needs practice. It has been known for some time from psychology experiments that practising a skill mentally is better than not practising at all, although obviously the best course of action is to combine physical with mental practice. But what is mental practice or imagery?

Mental practice is the repetition of a physical skill or movement sequence that is practised through thought and through pictures, rather than through actual physical movement. Although the exact reasons why mental imagery works are still not clearly understood, we do know that it does work. Experiments as long ago as the 1930s demonstrated that small electrical impulses could be detected in the muscles from thought alone. This suggests that the 'grooving in' of technique in sport can be accomplished, at least in part, by mental imagery. Obviously, such repetitive practice can only take place for predictable skills, such as spiking and setting. Although the situation will change each time in actuality, the general parameters of the skill remain the same. Equally, any predetermined moves can be mentally rehearsed to aid memory. It is more difficult, of course, to rehearse mentally the spontaneous movements that occur in an open team game such as volleyball. However, by visualising such open play and the options and decisions that you may take in such situations, your confidence may well be developed.

Brent Rushall, a sports psychologist, lists six important guidelines for successful mental rehearsal:

(i)   Your picture should be in the real environment. In other words, if you are wanting to practise competition spiking, then imagine yourself spiking in a competitive situation – it is more realistic.
(ii)   Perform the skill in full.
(iii)   Make sure the visualisation is successful – avoid rehearsing errors (although this is easier said than done!). With practice, though, you should improve the clarity of your mental image and find it easier to control.
(iv)   Visualise the skill before actual performance.
(v)   Imagine the skill at the normal speed.
(vi)   Imagine the skill visually and kinesthetically. In other words, try to feel the movement as if actually performing it. This is best done by visualising yourself actually performing rather than apparently watching yourself on a video. More useful advice can be found in John Syer and Christopher Connolly's book *Sporting Body, Sporting Mind*. They suggest that visualisation should follow these guidelines:

(i)   Start with relaxation.
(ii)   Stay alert.
(iii)   Use the present tense.
(iv)   Set realistic and specific goals (*see* later in this chapter).
(v)   Use all of your senses.
(vi)   Visualise at the correct speed.
(vii)   Practise regularly.
(viii) Enjoy it!

Answer the questionnaire in Fig 71 after your initial attempts at mental imagery. This should highlight some of your problem areas. Remember, keep the initial sessions short and relax beforehand.

Answer the following questions after each of your initial training sessions with mental imagery.

TICK ONE

	Yes	In Between	No
(i) Could you 'see' and 'feel' yourself perform the skill?			
(ii) Could you control the picture?			
(iii) Was the picture clear?			
(iv) Was the skill executed successfully?			
(v) Was the skill at normal speed?			
(vi) Did you stay relaxed?			
(vii) Did you stay alert?			
(viii) Did you use senses other than just 'sight' and 'feel'			

Fig 71 Mental imagery questionnaire.

Concentration and Mental Control

We all recognise the importance of concentration but rarely actually practise it as a skill. Try this exercise now but before doing so ensure that you have space around you – i.e. no furniture that you could hit if you fall over! (Also, it is best to have someone with you just in case you do start to fall over!)

(i)   Stand upright with hands on hips, eyes looking forward. Now take one foot off the ground and rest it against the other shin. How long can you keep your balance without moving the foot that is in contact with the ground?

(ii)   Try the same exercise again, this time with your eyes closed. How long can you keep balance this time?

(iii)   Finally, try it again, but this time close your eyes and tip your head back. How long can you keep your balance now?

It is probable that your balance deteriorated as you tried these exercises in turn. But why? These exercises each required concentration to maintain balance, but they became more difficult because they gave you less to concentrate on each time. The first exercise allowed you to have your eyes open, so balance was maintained by concentrating on a combination of seeing and feeling, and that is not very difficult because it is the way we operate in normal life. In the second exercise you were deprived of sight and so only had feeling to help you. If you did not concentrate totally on the small deviations of balance, you probably fell. Finally, in the third variation, the balance mechanisms (in the inner ear) were disturbed by tilting your head back and so – unless you could concentrate superbly on the limited feedback you were getting – you lost your balance easily.

What these exercises illustrate is that in sport, concentration is the ability to focus on the details around you that are needed for the game and to exclude those which are extraneous. In volleyball you need to focus your attention on the flight of the ball for your smash rather than the reaction of people watching on the sidelines. Many of the top sportspeople interviewed in David Hemery's book *The Pursuit of Sporting Excellence* rated concentration as a very important factor for them. A simple exercise to develop concentration is to sit, comfortable and relaxed in a chair, and to close your eyes. Then start counting each exhalation, starting at one and counting with each breath. You need to maintain a state of 'relaxed concentration' to get to the high numbers. Alternately, why not try the balance exercises again? Now that you know what to concentrate on you should be more successful.

Focusing Your Attention

Part of sports concentration, as already suggested, is the ability to attend to the right things at the right time. Fig 72 illustrates the process of attention in sport and shows that attention is made up of at least two parts – direction and focus. The direction of attention is the internal–external line on the diagram and refers to the extent we attend to things internally (i.e. thoughts and feelings) or externally (i.e. things in our environment). The other line in

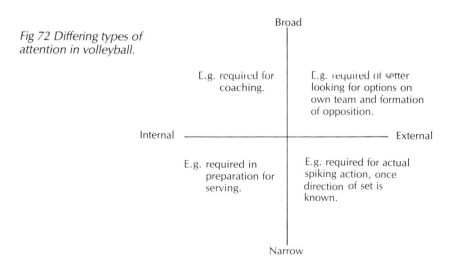

Fig 72 Differing types of attention in volleyball.

Broad

E.g. required for coaching.

E.g. required of setter looking for options on own team and formation of opposition.

Internal ———————————————— External

E.g. required in preparation for serving.

E.g. required for actual spiking action, once direction of set is known.

Narrow

Fig 72 is the focus or width of attention (broad–narrow) and refers to whether our attention is narrowly focused (e.g. on the ball) or broadly focused (e.g. on the changing defensive pattern of the opposition). Four main types of attention can therefore be deduced from Fig 72 and applied to different situations in volleyball.

The top left square is the broad–internal (analysis) style of attention required by the coach, who needs to be able to see things in a broad way – such as the way the entire team is functioning – but who at the same time focuses internally on his or her thoughts and feelings about the way the game is going, possible changes to be made and so on. The top right square is the broad–external (assessment) focus of attention often required by a setter in volleyball. For example, setters not only have to adjust to the way the ball is fed to them (requiring an external focus), but must also be aware of the opposition blockers and fellow spikers (broad focus).

The lower right square refers to the external–narrow (action) focus needed during the execution of a spike. This is because the attacker, once committed to the move, should focus on his or her own body movement and skill (narrow) as well as where the ball is to be placed on the other side of the net (external). Finally, the lower left square is internal–narrow and is the focus of attention needed for the preparation of a skill. In volleyball this might occur just prior to serving when attention should be focused narrowly on the exact skill itself. However, during the serve the attention should shift to a more external style.

An American psychologist, Robert Nideffer, who devised the model in Fig 72, suggests that it is not enough just to adopt the right focus of attention at the right time, but that it is also critical to be able to *shift* attention from one square to the next as appropriate. Many people in sport are unable to do this effectively because they have a 'preferred style' and tend to stick to it. Clearly, this leads to errors in the game and volleyball players and coaches should work on attentional focus and this ability to shift attention. For example, after a point has been played, the player could shift to an internal–narrow focus in order to control tension, and then quickly shift to a broad–external style to see where other players are positioned. Further details on this subject can be found in Nideffer's mental training manual listed at the end of this book.

Self-Confidence

Self-confidence is one of the key areas of mental training for sport. It is very rare indeed for successful sportspeople to have a persistent lack of self-confidence. In understanding self-confidence, four main factors need to be identified. These are: prior performance; demonstration and imitation; verbal persuasion and positive self-talk; monitoring arousal. The most powerful source of confidence is likely to be your past performances and since success will lead to confidence and confidence to success, a 'positive confidence cycle' can be set up. If your sports performance is improving then all is fine, but what can you do when your performance is declining? How can you break in to the confidence cycle? One technique which has been shown to be effective is goal-setting (to be considered later in this section).

The second source of confidence is observation and imitation of others. Coaches can organise highly effective learning situations for volleyball players through the use of demonstrations, films and so forth which can act as confidence-building sessions. For example, a player lacking confidence in serving may benefit from watching someone perform the skill success-fully. (However, it is not *always* such a good idea to constantly show the 'ideal' skill executed by the best player, as this can sometimes deflate confidence with players saying to themselves 'I'll never be able to do it like that!') Live and recorded demonstrations have been found to be effective, as well as techniques which physically assist players to adopt the correct positions. This is more usual in sports such as gymnastics but can be used for some of the volleyball skills. In addition, players may build confidence through imagining correct skills, so highlighting again the importance of mental imagery.

A third source of confidence is verbal persuasion from others, although this may be a relatively weak source of confidence, depending on the people involved; certainly encouragement from a highly respected person can help. A better source of persuasion is likely to come from *within* the player. Confidence-building statements are sometimes referred to as 'positive self-talk' or 'affirmations'. The most famous one in sport is Mohammed Ali's 'I am the greatest!' Although it may sound odd, there are

Technique	Method	Comments
'As if' visualisation	Imagine you are someone or something which creates confidence for you. Example: imagine that you are ten feet tall when spiking or blocking.	You can add a positive slogan (*see* below) to go with this exercise.
Positive slogans	Think of a slogan which, when you see it, gives you confidence and direction.	Write it on a card and keep it in a prominent place.
Special words	Think of key or special words which are likely to help confidence, such as 'SLAM!' as you spike, or 'ENVELOP' as you block.	

Fig 73 Techniques for developing confidence through words and images.

plenty of examples of people gaining confidence from saying positive things to themselves. Three techniques for developing positive self-talk and affirmations are given in Fig 73.

A further source of self-confidence can be found in the physiological arousal of the body. If the stress response (referred to earlier) is thought to indicate negative feelings such as fear, then arousal will reduce confidence. The typical reaction here would be for the server, at a critical time in the game, to say, 'I can feel my heart pounding. Hell, I'm scared!' Conversely, if the person sees his or her reaction differently, it could become a positive influence. For example, the server could say, 'I can feel my heart pounding. That's great! I'm ready for this!' Changing such negative thoughts into positive ones can be a useful confidence strategy.

Goal-Setting

One of the best ways to develop confidence and build sound psychological principles into your training is to use goal-setting. Although many people in sport use some kind of planning which approximates to the setting of goals, probably little thought has gone into the best way of utilising goal-setting. Before outlining a simple goal-setting exercise for volleyball players, the following guidelines should be noted:

(i)   Goals can be set for the short term, medium term or long term. To help immediate motivation and action, short term goals are best.
(ii)   Goals should be specific and measurable. Just to set the goal of 'improving my serve' does not give enough direction. Set a goal that is highly specific and can be measured for success. Feedback based on such measurements is crucial for successful goal-setting.
(iii)   Goals should be realistic, but challenging. It is easy to set very high goals, but disappointment will set in if they are not reached. On the other hand, very easy goals will not create extra motivation and direction.
(iv)   Goals should be accepted and worth while. For goals to be effective they must be accepted by the participant (hence it is best for the player to be involved in the goal-setting process rather than simply the coach), and considered worth the effort involved.

Fig 74 shows you a goal-setting example for a volleyball player. Study this and then complete your own using the structure in Fig 75.

Team-Work

The final topic for mental training that will be considered here refers to team-work. There is no magic formula for getting teams to work well together, although some guidelines may help. Further details can be found in *Sporting Body, Sporting Mind* by Syer and Connolly.

Long term goal	Goals for next month	Goals and action for this week
To be the number one setter in the club.	To learn the hook serve so that at least eight out of ten serves are successful.	(i) To spend ten mins each session practising the hook serve with emphasis on varying trajectory. (ii) To hit designated floor spaces with at least eight out of ten serves.
To be selected for county team.	To improve the forward dive to ensure safe and effective landing.	(i) To spend five mins each session on the forward dive. (ii) To retrieve at least six out of ten balls using a safe landing technique and static feed from coach.

Fig 74 Examples of goal-setting in volleyball.

Long term goal	Goals for next month	Goals and action for this week
		(i) (ii)
		(i) (ii)
		(i) (ii)

Fig 75 Your goal-setting chart.

Understanding Others

A key to effective team-work is understanding why other people are playing the game – it may come as a surprise that people do not play volleyball for the same reasons. Three main types of reasons have been identified in the past:

(i)   To play to win.
(ii) To play well and demonstrate skill.
(iii) To be part of a team.

Clearly these reasons will exist in players in varying degrees and some may be interested in all three aspects. Nevertheless, coaches, team leaders etc. may find that knowing their colleagues' main reasons for playing could help relationships within the team and between players and coaches. For example, the player wanting to demonstrate skills will be far less tolerant of sitting on the bench during a game than the person who is happy just being a team member.

Team Togetherness

It is often assumed that teams that are cohesive will play better. Although there have been exceptions, this is generally true. However, the cohesion of the team is not a simple matter: players have different personalities and will react differently in various situations. The group 'psych-up', therefore, is likely only to work for some of the players.

It is best to view group cohesion in two ways. Firstly, the extent to which players view the team as a whole (i.e. cohesion, togetherness, unity etc.) and secondly, the degree of attraction the individual player has to the group. Both of these can have two 'orientations', or ways of working – task and social. A task orientation is where the focus is on getting the job done. This would mean that the team is primarily motivated to play well and to win, rather than to enjoy each others' company. A social orientation, on the other hand, is geared towards social relationships rather than group performance. One would expect a social orientation to be stronger in more 'casual' teams and a task orientation to be stronger in high-level or professional teams, although there is no reason why most teams should not possess an interest in both orientations to some degree.

Team Meetings

John Syer and Christopher Connolly have identified three types of team meeting that may be useful in developing mental skills for teams:

(i)   Pre-competition meetings. These are for the team to warm up in the emotional and psychological sense. They should be short and to the point. However, not all players will want the highly excitable 'psych-up' favoured in rugby changing rooms, so coaches or team captains who conduct such meetings should be careful.

(ii)   Post-competition discussion meetings. These are held at the training session after a competition to discuss the team's performance and to plan for the future. Group goal-setting can take place here.

(iii)   Team-spirit meetings. Numerous discussion topics may be aired although this meeting will probably not take place very often.

One aspect of mental training that should help the team effort is that if every player in the team makes a commitment to mental training, then this in itself should assist the cohesiveness and 'togetherness' of the team.

POSTSCRIPT

Thus we see that mental training provides a positive step forward towards becoming a 'complete' volleyball player. Everyone will be doing it in the years to come, so why not get a 'head start'?

6 Summary and Programme Planning

In this book we have attempted to provide coverage of the major areas of training for volleyball. These are:

(i)   Skill development.
(ii) Physical fitness.
(iii) Nutrition.
(iv) Injury prevention.
(v)   Mental training.

Of course it is not easy to fit all of these into a day-to-day training programme. However, each of these should form part of the regular ongoing training programme and two in particular – injury prevention and nutrition – should underpin each session, rather than being training sessions in their own right. So, having acquired this wisdom, you now need some guidelines for implementing the programme.

ASSESSMENT

A useful start is to assess your current level of training and performance. Only then can a proper 'prescription' and planning exercise take place. For example, assessment may show that you are relatively weak in leg power and in the skill of digging. These would then feature more extensively in your training programme. On a more general level, the training plan should follow the following structure:

(I)   End of season recovery.
(ii) Preparation phase I (out of season).
(iii) Preparation phase II (pre-season).
(iv) Competition phase.

The emphasis in each phase is shown in Fig 76. This outlines no more than a basic plan and it is likely that different players will have to adapt this to meet their own needs. However, in terms of 'peaking', league matches prevent this being a desirable or attainable strategy. In leagues, early season form needs to be high and then maintained. However, for cup competition it is possible to build up to a peak nearer the latter stages of the event. If this is the case then the emphasis should shift back to period 3 (preparation

Training component	PERIOD			
	1	2	3	4
Mental training		**	***	***
Aerobic training		**	*	*
Strength		***	**	*
Muscular endurance		***	**	**
Power		*	***	**
Speed	[rest or diversion from volleyball]	*	***	***
Flexibility		**	**	**
Individual skills		***	***	***
Team skills		*	**	***

Period 1 End of season recovery (up to 2 weeks).
Period 2 Preparatory phase I, out of season (up to 2 months).
Period 3 Preparatory phase II, pre-season (up to 2 months).
Period 4 Competition phase (up to 8 months).

*** very important
 ** important
  * lower priority (maintenance)

Fig 76 Planning your training throughout the year.

phase II) for the early rounds to peaking in period 4 (the competition phase). Do not try to stay with the training schedules of period 4 for too long as staleness or 'burn-out' may occur.

It is usual to change the pattern of training throughout the year to get the best results when they are most needed. This is called 'periodisation' or 'cycling' the training year by doing different exercises at different times. The main reasons for using periodisation are:

(i) . To vary the training load.
(ii)   To aid recovery.
(iii) To achieve peak performance at a desired time.

This is particularly important for more advanced players who need to peak for specific matches, although beginners, too, should have variety in training.

A BALANCED PROGRAMME

A balanced training programme is important for all volleyball players. The game itself requires skill, fitness, mental skills, and many more qualities.

Level	Physical fitness	Skill training	Mental training
Beginner and club player	Foundation principles across all components.	Basic individual techniques; later team skills for the club player.	Relaxation, arousal control and goal-setting.
County and regional player	Basic components plus emphasis on weaknesses and special needs.	Development of advanced skills.	Problem-solving skills.
National and international player	Specialised intensive training.	Maintenance and development of individual skills; advanced group skills.	Self-sufficiency in mental skills; advanced individual techniques.

Fig 77 Training patterns for volleyball players of different levels.

This means that your training must also reflect such diverse needs; Fig 77 shows how the 'playing level' might affect the training.

CONCLUSION

There is no such player as the 'complete volleyballer'! However, it is to be hoped that you can get closer to fulfilling your own goals of personal improvement and enjoyment through a higher standard of volleyball by implementing the training ideas from this book.

Glossary

Aerobic   'With oxygen'; used to describe 'steady-state' exercise where the body relies on oxygen as a continuous source of fuel.

Amenorrhoea   Absence of normal female monthly cycle or periods.

Amino Acid   The constituent parts of protein: eight of these acids cannot be made in the body (these are termed essential) and must form part of our diet. Another twelve can by synthesised in the body.

Anaemia   A deficiency of red blood cells, or of their haemoglobin. Most likely to occur in women with heavy periods or otherwise due to insufficient iron replacement.

Anaerobic   'Without oxygen'; used to describe the energy systems of the body which are used in short, high-intensity exercise.

Attack Line   A line in each half drawn across the width of the court parallel to the net 3m from the centre line.

Attack Zone   The area between the attack line and the centre line. A back court player may not direct the ball from within the attack zone into the opponents' court, unless the ball is below net height when struck. If the player takes off behind the attack line he or she may hit the ball in any way and at any height before landing in the attack area.

Back Court   The area of court between the base line and the attack line – normally occupied by players in positions 1, 6 and 5 at the time of service.

Back Line Player   Players in Positions 1, 6 or 5 at the time of service.

Basal Metabolic Rate   A term used to describe the absolute amount of energy required to maintain the body function for life. It is a very precise measure made when the subject is awake, at perfect rest, 12 hours after a meal and in a thermoneutral environment.

Block   The block is the counter to the smash. The opposing players jump up and place a wall of hands in the path of the smashed ball with the intention of blocking its path across the net. Only front court players may block.

Body Mass Index (BMI)   A convenient way to express the ratio of height to weight and give a simple estimate of abnormal weight for height. BMI is weight (kilograms) divided by the height (metres) squared and should lie in the range 17–25.

Caffeine   A drug found in tea, coffee, chocolate and some carbonated beverages. Promotes fatty acid release, affects the cardiovascular system and is a diuretic.

Calorie   A very small, precisely defined unit of heat. One thousand calories are equivalent to one kilocalorie or kcal.

Carbohydrates   Molecules containing carbon, hydrogen and oxygen. They may be small simple units, often sweet, such as glucose, sucrose or larger units, often tasteless, such as starch. We cannot digest all carbohydrates and some are termed 'unavailable'; these include cellulose (dietary fibre). Carbohydrates provide energy for the body, about 4kcals per gram or 120kcals per ounce.

Cardiorespiratory Exercise   Exercise such as running, cycling, swimming, or any exercise utilising large muscle groups for an extended period of time; develops the ability of the blood, heart, lungs and other systems of the body to persist in work.

Combination Attack   Two or more players will approach the net at approximately the same time. The opposing blockers will not be sure which of the players will make the attack, what kind of attack it will be and from what position in court.

Cool-Down   A period of light exercise and stretching after vigorous activity.

Covering the Smash   When a player is smashing the ball his or her team-mates come closer to the player in case the block sends the ball back into their court. They will then be in a good position to play the ball before it touches the ground.

Dehydration   Loss of body fluid with inadequate replacement. Liable to result from excessive sweating, diarrhoea or vomiting.

Dietary Deficiency   Inadequate intake of an essential nutrient which results in reduced body stores of the nutrient and eventually affects body function. Diagnosis of a deficiency requires biochemical tests.

Dietary Fibre   That part of our food which is not digested by our normal digestive juices and therefore remains in the intestine providing bulk. However, dietary fibre *is* largely digested by organisms in the large bowel and as such can be absorbed to provide energy.

Dig or Bump Pass   The ball is played on the outstretched forearms. This pass is used when the ball is travelling fast or very low.

Dislocation   A displacement of the bony surfaces at a joint so that the ends of the bones do not meet, or meet incorrectly. Requires immediate referral to a doctor.

Doping   The use of substances which artificially improve or augment an athlete's performance.

Fats   Molecules containing carbon, hydrogen and oxygen. The small molecules are called fatty acids and dietary fats are a mixture of different fatty acids often held together by another molecule of glycerol and are then referred to simply as fat. Fats provide energy, 9kcals per gram or 270kcals per ounce.

First Pass   The pass made, on receive of the serve or smash, to the setter.

Flexibility   A component of physical fitness or form of exercise which refers to the stretching of muscles.

Front Court   The area of court between the centre line and the attack line – normally occupied by players in positions 2, 3 and 4 at the time of service.

Front Court Player   One of the players in Position 2, 3 or 4 at the time of service.

Glycogen   The form in which the mammalian body stores carbohydrate. It is mainly stored in the liver and muscles and constitutes a very mobile but limited store of energy for the body. It can be used without the presence of oxygen, i.e. anaerobically.

Haemoglobin   The oxygen-carrying component of red blood cells composed of an iron-based substance.

Isokinetic   A form of resistance training where a machine provides resistance which allows for constant limb speed.

Isometric   A form of resistance training where no movement takes place.

Isotonic   A form of resistance training involving the lifting of free-standing objects, such as barbells.

Joule   A very small and precise measure of the amount of work. The energy in food is related to the amount of work it can generate and therefore sometimes the energy value of food is expressed in joules. One thousand joules form one kilojoule or kJ. One kcal is equivalent to 4.2kJ.

Jump Volley   A volley pass played with the player airborne – often used as an attacking shot, or to initiate a fast attack.

Lead Blocker   The player who sets the line and timing of the block – normally the outside blocker when countering a wing attack.

Ligaments   Strong bands of fibrous tissue which bind bones together at a joint.

Mental Imagery   The process of practising a skill in your mind rather than through physical practice.

Minerals   Inert substances some of which are essential to the body for its functioning. Calcium, magnesium, sodium, potassium, phosphorus, iron and zinc are some of these essential minerals.

Muscular Endurance   The ability to contract a muscle, or group of muscles, continuously over time.

Nutrients   Those parts of food which are used by the body to allow functioning of cells. Carbohydrates and fats are 'burned' to provide energy for cells to work – internally in order to make more tissue, for example, and externally to propel the body. Protein, vitamins and minerals are all used by the cells to function normally.

Osteoarthritis   The surfaces of bones at a joint are covered in cartilage which may become worn away, particularly in a joint which has been previously damaged. The joint may be painful, swollen and stiff.

Osteoporosis   A condition, mainly in women, in which the bones become increasingly thin and brittle – it is caused by reduced sex hormones and possibly low intake of calcium.

Overload   System in which training is progressively increased.

Power   The combination of strength and speed.

Progressive Muscle Relaxation (PMR)   A form of relaxation training which teaches the recognition of tension and relaxation through a series of muscle–tension exercises.

Proprioceptive Neuromusclar Facilitation (PNF) A form of flexibility training which requires the muscle to be contracted before stretching.

Protein That part of the food which contains amino acids. It can be used for energy and provides 4kcals per gram or 120kcals per ounce.

Rally The complete unit of play from the service until play is stopped by the referee and a point is awarded.

Reaction Time The time which elapses between the stimulus and the start of the movement in response to the stimulus.

Reverse Volley A volley pass played overhead to send the ball behind the volleyer   often used to deceive the opposition.

Rotation On regaining service, teams rotate one position clockwise so that a new player comes to the serving position.

Serve The act of putting the ball into play by the player in position 1 from behind the base line.

Service Area A 3m channel of indefinite length is formed by the extension of the right sideline and the serving line, which is marked 3m from this sideline. The server must be in this area when the ball is played.

Set Pass This is the volley pass which is played near to and above the net for the smasher to hit.

Setter The player whose job it is to play the set pass. A specialist player is normally used because the job is demanding and requires a high level of skill.

Shoot Set Sometimes known as the parallel set. It is played fast and low across the court for the smasher to hit. When timed effectively it results in a very fast attack.

Short Set A set played near to the setter and only a short distance above the net. This is also a very fast method of attacking.

Skinfold Thickness The layer of body fat lying directly beneath the skin which can be measured using skinfold callipers. This layer of fat is related to total body fat which may be estimated from this method.

Smash The main attacking shot in the game where the high ball is hit powerfully over the net downwards towards the opposition's court.

Smasher The more common name for the spiker – the player whose job it is to complete the attack by hitting the ball across the net.

Sorbothane A synthetic substance which absorbs energy well and is used as a 'shock-absorber' for inserts into shoes, mainly at the heel.

Spiker The American term for smasher.

Sports Anaemia Probably not a true anaemia; the increase in plasma volume brought on by a serious training schedule dilutes the red cells reducing their concentration, the total number of red cells remaining the same.

Sprain An injury to the ligaments around a joint which may produce pain, swelling and discolouration.

Strength The ability of the muscle to exert force.

Stress Fracture A minute crack in a bone due to repeated overloading by an inappropriately rapid increase in training loads.

Switching   The technique of changing the positions of players during the rally so that a more effective line-up is obtained.

Tendon   White 'cords' which attach muscles to bones. They may become inflamed (tendonitis), partially torn, or completely broken (ruptured tendon).

Tonicity of Fluid   The concentration of particles in a solution compared to the concentration of particles in body fluids, especially blood. If the concentration in a solution is greater than blood it is termed hypertonic; if lower in concentration, hypotonic. Water will always travel from a less concentrated solution to a more concentrated solution.

Variable Resistance Training   A form of resistance training which varies the loading to accommodate the mechanical efficiency of the body levers so that optimal tension is placed on the muscle throughout the whole range of movement.

Vitamins   Molecules which are found in food and are essential to cells for their efficient functioning. Some vitamins are associated and soluble in fat (vitamins A, D, E, K), others are soluble in water (Vitamins B and C).

Volley Pass   The main pass in the game. It is played on the fingers of both hands simultaneously in such a way that the ball does not come to rest.

Warm-Up   Light, mainly aerobic and flexibility exercises prior to vigorous activity.

Zone   The zones on court are those areas corresponding to the positions occupied by players 1, 2, 3, 4, 5, and 6. *See* below:

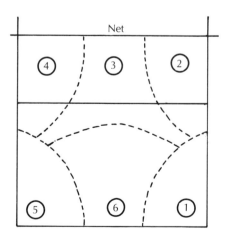

Further Reading

GAME SKILLS

Nicholls, K., *Volleyball* (The Crowood Press, 1986)*

PHYSICAL FITNESS

Anderson, B., *Stretching* (Pelham, 1980)
Fox, E., *Sports Physiology* (Saunders College, 1979)
Hazeldine, R., *Fitness for Sport* (The Crowood Press, 1985)*
Lear, P.J., *Weight Training* (A & C Black, 1988)
National Coaching Foundation, *Physiology and Performance* (1986)
National Strength and Conditioning Association Journal

NUTRITION

DHSS, *Recommended Amounts of Food Energy and Nutrients for Groups of People in the UK* (Report on Health and Social Subjects No. 15, 1979)
Eisenmann, P. and Johnson D., *Coaches' Guide to Nutrition and Weight Control* (Human Kinetics, 1982)
Haskell, W. *et al.*, *Nutrition and Athletic Performance* (Bull Publishing, 1982)
Ministry of Agriculture, Fisheries and Food, *Manual of Nutrition* (HMSO, 1985)
Paul, A. and Southgate, D., *McCance and Widdowson's 'The Composition of Foods'* (HMSO, 1978)

SPORTS INJURIES

Grisogono, V., *Sports Injuries: a Self-Help Guide* (John Murray, 1983)*
National Coaching Foundation, *Safety First for Coaches* (1986)
Read, M. and Wade P., *Sports and Medicine* (Butterworth, 1981)
St John Ambulance, *First Aid Manual* (Dorling Kindersley, 1982)

MENTAL TRAINING

National Coaching Foundation, *The Coach at Work* (1986)
Nideffer, R.M., *The Athlete's Guide to Mental Training* (Human Kinetics, 1985)
Railo, W., *Willing to Win* (Springfield Books, 1986)
Syer, J. and Connolly, C., *Sporting Body, Sporting Mind* (Cambridge University Press, 1984)*
Terry, P., *The Winning Mind* (Thorsons, 1989)

MISCELLANEOUS

Hemery, D., *The Pursuit of Sporting Excellence* (Collins Willow, 1986)

*particularly recommended

Useful Addresses

British Amateur Weight Lifters' Association, 3 Iffley Turn, Oxford OX4 4DY.

British Association of Sports Sciences, c/o National Coaching Foundation (*see* below).

English Volleyball Association, 27 South Road, West Bridgford, Nottingham NG2 7AG.

National Coaching Foundation, 4 College Close, Beckett Park, Leeds LS6 3QH.

National Strength & Conditioning Association, P.O. Box 81410, Lincoln, Nebraska 68501, USA.

Northern Ireland Volleyball Association, House of Sport, Upper Malone Road, Belfast BT9 5LA.

Scottish Volleyball Association, Castlecliff, 25 Johnson Terrace, Edinburgh EH1 2NH.

Sports Council, 16 Upper Woburn Place, London WC1H 0QP.

St John Ambulance, Supplies Department, Priory House, St John's Gate, Clerkenwell, London EC1M 4DA.

Welsh Volleyball Association, 112 St Fagan's Road, Fairwater, Cardiff, CF5 3AN.

Index